GET BACK
to Work!

GET BACK to Work!

A No-Nonsense Guide
For Finding Your Next Job Fast

Charles Grossner ● Leo Spindel ● Harvey Glasner

Fitzhenry & Whiteside

Get Back To Work!

Fitzhenry and Whiteside Limited
195 Allstate Parkway
Markham, Ontario L3R 4T8

In the United States:
121 Harvard Avenue, Suite 2
Allston, Massachusetts 02134

www.fitzhenry.ca godwit@fitzhenry.ca

Fitzhenry & Whiteside acknowledges with thanks the Canada Council for the Arts, the Government of Canada through its Book Publishing Industry Development Program, and the Ontario Arts Council for their support of our publishing program.

10 9 8 7 6 5 4 3 2 1

National Library of Canada Cataloguing-in-Publication
Grossner, Charles, 1946-
Get back to work : a no-nonsense guide for finding your next job fast / Charles Grossner, Leo Spindel, Harvey Glasner.
Includes index.
ISBN 1-55041-741-X
1. Job hunting. 2. Career development. I. Spindel, Leo II. Glasner, Harvey III. Title.
HF5382.7.G76 2002   650.14   C2002-902683-0

United States Cataloging-in-Publication Data
Grossner, Charles.
  Get back to work : a no nonsense guide for finding your next job fast / Charles Grossner, Leo Spindel, Harvey Glasner. --1st ed.
[150] p. : ill. ; cm.
Includes index.
Summary: A how to guide, designed to lead the user down the path of least resistance to a better job, based upon the best practices of top career management firms from around the world.

ISBN 1-55041-741-X (pbk.)

1. Job hunting. I. Spindel, Leo. II. Glasner, Harvey. III. Title.
650.14 21   CIP   HF5382.7.G76 2002

Design by Darrell McCalla
Printed and bound in Canada

Contents

Step 2:
Find Your Best Fit

Step 3:
Building the Perfect Beast

Step 4:
Launch Your Marketing Campaign

Step 5:
Ace The Interview

Acknowledgments

We are indebted to the hundreds of job search and career transition candidates who have shared their personal experiences, successes and frustrations with us. Without their insight into the dynamic of the job search and career transition process, this book would not have been possible.

We also wish to acknowledge Marianne Rapicano whose hours of effort took a manuscript authored by three individuals and wove it into a singular voice. To Steve Naumovski, a sincere thank you for assisting with pre-publication drafts. To our colleagues at PeopleFind Inc, we appreciate your support and patience. To our wives and children, thank you for your understanding while we put in the many hours to complete this work. To all the folks at Fitzhenry & Whiteside, thank you for believing in us. And, a special thank you to our editor, Richard Dionne, who helped us fine tune the manuscript while keeping us focused on our task.

Welcome

Congratulations, you're at a crossroads. You can travel down a more rewarding career path or you can become paralyzed by inertia and fear.

This guide is the helping hand you need to lead you down the path of least resistance to a better job. It has been prepared by experienced, sensitive professionals who are involved in Psychology, Communications, Recruiting, Personal Development and Career Coaching. We have examined and assessed the best practices of top career management firms from around the world. Then, we synthesized these practices into a step-by-step process designed to give you optimal results—fast.

You may be in your fifties and suddenly on the job market after many years of employment in one firm; you may be in your thirties or forties and in the prime of your career; you may be a retiree looking for a second career; or a senior not ready to retire; a mother wanting to re-enter the job market; a recent graduate with limited years of work experience; or a recent arrival from abroad looking for employment. No matter who you are, or what position you may be in, if you're looking for a new job—this book will help you find your way.

> *It's choice, not chance that determines your destiny.*
> Jean Nidetch

You may be on the market as a result of adverse market conditions, competitive factors or you may have experienced downsizing due to technological change; your position may have been rationalized after an acquisition or merger, or you may have been "squeezed out" as a result of conflict or personality differences (politics). You may currently be employed but in a situation where working conditions or anticipated changes warrant a move. You may be in a situation where you are successfully employed but for personal, ideological, or economic reasons, still feel the need to pursue a new career. Regardless, you will require a process and a plan to find new employment. This book is intended to provide clear direction and successful strategies on how to go about this task.

The job search process can be a traumatic and unwelcome event that brings high stress to you and those around you. Our aim is to harness your emotions and turn them into powerful forces that will help you define your goals and achieve your desires. At the same time, we'll give you practical methods for sharpening your search skills, writing stand-out resumés, and developing winning interview techniques.

> *Remember this also, and be well persuaded of its truth: the future is not in the hands of Fate, but in ours.*
>
> Jean Jules Jusserand

You could spend a terribly long time in an unfocused state, sending out ineffectual letters and wallowing in self-doubt. Or, you could work through our proven six-step process. It's quick and effective, and will take you to that new job or career:

Step 1:
Take Control of Your Transition

Recognize your emotions and turn them into positive energy in your pursuit of a new job or career. Separate feelings from actions so you can successfully manage the ups and downs of the job search process.

Step 2:
Find Your Best Fit

Define your skills and develop a comprehensive list of accomplishments. This critical self-discovery and esteem-building exercise will help reinforce your confidence, define your goals, and effectively position yourself going forward.

Step 3:
Building the Perfect Beast

Build a strong resumé based on your accomplishments and USP (Unique Selling Proposition). Learn how to avoid common errors, identify positive references and produce material that will help you launch your marketing campaign.

Step 4:
Launch Your Marketing Campaign

Market yourself as a "brand," linking your features and benefits to target-specific opportunities. Network effectively, deal with headhunters, respond to ads and tap the hidden job market so you can generate interviews with the right people in the organizations you target.

> *A brand is a promise to deliver on your features and benefits.*

Step 5:
Ace The Interview

The key to the job search process is the interview. Each interview within a target organization is a critical passage to the next step. Become familiar with the various types of interviews and the essential non-verbal skills you will need to demonstrate.

Step 6:
Negotiate The Offer

Learn the ins and outs of job negotiation. Recognize the pitfalls that can undermine a positive campaign. Understand the tools required to negotiate an offer agreeable to both you and the employer.

Our method is here and our support is near. And the best news so far is that you've already chosen to succeed.

> *Let us never negotiate out of fear. But let us never fear to negotiate.*
> *John F. Kennedy*

So let's get down to business.

STEP 1:
Take Control of Your Transition

You're a manager with 20 years of progressive and continuous work experience and you suddenly find yourself out of work.

You're a highly trained technician in a specialized industry where market conditions have changed and led to a reduction in the workforce—you're now unemployed with no prospect of returning to your field.

> **Happiness belongs to the self sufficient.**
> *Aristotle*

You're a stay-at-home parent who wants to return to the workforce after a five-year absence.

You took early retirement and find yourself bored to death and want to work again.

You're a newcomer to the country with a professional designation yet you find your credentials not fully recognized.

You're a recent graduate with limited or no experience in your preferred field and you're in a Catch-22.

So you're in job search mode, a two-pronged process of discovery. You'll examine yourself, your attitudes and beliefs about working. Next, you'll examine the job market to see where your skills and experiences fit with current demand.

You will face barriers. You may face prejudice. You may feel anxious. You may feel rejected. You may be frozen by fear and self-doubt. You may not know the local protocol. Bottom line, you need to overcome your fears, surmount the barriers and move forward with confidence.

Each one of us represents a value proposition (a set of distinguishing features and benefits) and it is incumbent upon us to understand and leverage that proposition in order to obtain the desired objective—that is, a new job, a new career, a new opportunity.

While working through this job search process, you'll discover valuable methods that can be used anytime you want to switch jobs, with the least amount of angst and in the shortest time possible.

So You've Lost Your Job

Up until now, your destiny may have been decided by people and forces outside of your control. Now you're in a position to take back command and conduct a systematic job search that leads to a more rewarding and fulfilling career.

Separate feelings from actions

You did not expect to lose your job and it may have come at the worst possible time. Naturally, there are many emotions swirling around you: disappointment, guilt, fear. But it's important to keep those emotions at bay while you get on with the business of exploring your next opportunity.

We're not asking you to deny that you're feeling anxious, isolated or depressed. But we are asking you to separate these feelings from the concrete steps you'll need to take you to the next level. In fact, "compartmentalization" will be an important new skill you'll learn as you work through the get *back to work* process.

> *The game of life is a lot like football. You have to tackle your problems, block your fears and score your points when you get the opportunity.*
>
> Lewis Grizzard

Without doubt, losing a job ranks right up there on the stress meter with losing a loved one. And it may take months, even years to completely come to terms with it. While you're looking for your next job, you can talk openly with a career coach or psychologist who can help you see things in a more objective light. *Is life always so unfair? Do I bear some responsibility for what happened? Am I a bad provider, a bad parent?* Whatever your thoughts, a talk with a respected counselor might help you gain some valuable insights into your own personality, your field of endeavor and the way the world so often turns.

But this is a side issue. Your immediate task is to accept your transition, regain control, and make the most of this change in the fastest time possible.

Recognize your emotions

You've lost more than a job—you've lost part of your identity. So let's deal with this issue and get past it. Like many people, you probably invested a great deal of your self-image in what you do for a living. But you are not what you do. You are a valuable and complex individual with unique talents and experiences, who happens to work as a marketing manager, mechanic, school teacher, bank president or whatever.

Now's the time to reap the rewards of your special skills and knowledge and use them to get back in the game. Remember, you haven't lost anything that makes you who you really are. No one can take away the education and success that's already on your resume. You're simply moving from one chapter of your life to the next.

> *Life can only be understood backwards. But it must be lived forwards.*
>
> Soren Kierkegaard

There are a number of natural—but negative—emotions that bubble up when you leave a job. Recognize them. Give yourself permission to feel them. Then challenge them. Most are irrational thoughts that can rob you of your spirit and productivity when you need these most.

Angry? You have a right to be mad. You've lost self-respect, income and a social structure that defined your life. Go ahead and punch a heavybag.

Confused? It doesn't make sense? It's not clear why you had to leave? The future is uncertain? Go ahead and vent to a good friend.

Shamed? You're embarrassed. You feel like a failure. Go ahead and look at your diplomas, achievements and awards. They're still there.

Frightened? How will you support yourself and your family? Go ahead and examine your financial resources and options with your bank manager. Develop an interim plan to get over this rough patch.

Betrayed? You gave them your best and they dumped you. Or they made it impossible for you to stay. Go ahead and hug your dog, your family and everyone else who loves you.

Helpless? You're overwhelmed and things have spun out of control. Go ahead and dust off your resumé. Set up an office. Send your suits to the dry cleaners. Get busy and stay active.

> *Always forgive your enemies. Nothing annoys them so much.*
> Oscar Wilde

Inadequate? Worried that you're washed up and out of date? Afraid you lack the skills to compete in today's job market? Go ahead and scan the courses available at local colleges and resource centers.

Relieved? You may have been unhappy for a long time and now you're free. Go ahead and take a long walk. Relax. Treat yourself to a cappuccino. Do nothing for an afternoon. You've earned it.

Get on with the grieving process

No one is immune to death and dying. No one goes through life always healthy. No one hits a home run every time at bat. Loss, in all its forms, is a natural part of life. So it's wise to understand the grieving process and work through it, especially when you lose something as important as a job.

> *The only cure for grief is action.*
> George Henry Lewes

Here are the classic stages of grief. You may go through each in a different order and you may linger longer at one stage than at another. Nevertheless, our advice is simple: *don't hold back!* Allow yourself to feel and express your emotions in a safe place with sympathetic people. But never express your grief in a job interview. If you're particularly angry or depressed, postpone it. Call your doctor. Get medication and counseling if you need it. Start your interviews when you're feeling better.

STAGES OF GRIEF

Shock It hasn't sunk in yet.

Denial "I can't believe this is happening."

Relief "Finally, a burden has been lifted."

Anger You blame those you think are responsible, including yourself.

Depression You lose interest in life. Note: if you are lingering at this stage, see your doctor. He or she has concrete solutions. Remember, a doctor is a vital link in your support network.

Acceptance You've come to grips with your loss. Now you have the energy and desire to move forward. Acceptance is the ultimate goal in transcending your grief.

Know the flow

Losing a job—traumatic on the one hand—needs to be placed in proper perspective. You can view it as a major setback or as an exciting opportunity to move forward. This concept is very well expressed by William Bridges, author of *Transitions: Making Sense of Life's Changes*. Bridges examines the natural progression from Ending to Neutral Zone to New Beginning. It's a journey, and you're moving from one place to the next, headed for a destination. If you recognize what's happening along the way, you can dictate, to a large degree, what your final destination will be. Here are some of Bridges's insights into the process of life change and how you may be feeling, en route.

> *There will come a time when you believe everything is finished. That will be the beginning.*
>
> Louis L'Amour

Endings

As soon as an ending to one stage in your life occurs, a transition begins. To make a transition to something better,
you must let go of your old reality and old identity. You may experience the following emotions in the process:

DISENGAGEMENT

- There is a separation from your previous role and identity. This experience may have been thrust upon you, or you may have initiated the change.
- Feelings of separation are often magnified by events such as divorce, illness or death.
- Endings lead to transitions. Transitions lead to New Beginnings. Endings are a gift and a message for you to move on.
- Don't be afraid. Accept the fact that something is lost and may never come back. But always remember something else is waiting for you. Stay focused on going after it.

> *People often say that this or that person has not found himself. But the self is not something that one finds. It is something one creates.*
>
> Thomas Szasz

DISIDENTIFICATION

- Your old job gave you recognition, status, and social and psychological bonds.
- It also gave you a sense of purpose. It bolstered your self-esteem.
- Don't worry, your identity is still intact. Being out of work doesn't change who you are. You simply have to give yourself new goals.
- Like they say in the clothing trade, it's "out with the old and in with the new."

DISENCHANTMENT

- You were betrayed by those you trusted.
- Your old assumptions and beliefs are no longer valid. Perhaps they were never realistic in the first place. Yet you

held onto them anyway because they worked for you at the time.

- Feelings of disenchantment will pass once you accept them and start making positive changes.
- If you continue to deny your feelings, you'll become disillusioned. You'll increase the likelihood of repeating the past. You'll miss this opportunity to examine yourself for the better.

DISORIENTATION

- You feel like you're up the creek without a paddle.
- You feel lost, confused and without a sense of direction.
- You have plenty of time but no vision of the future.
- You must seize the opportunity to begin anew. Have faith in yourself and the future.
- Things will change. Doors will open.
- You must be willing to scrutinize yourself. *Where have I been? Where am I headed?*

Neutral Zones

This is the middle phase, in between your Ending and New Beginning. Yes, it's fraught with anxiety, but it's also rich with challenges. Working through this stage is like maneuvering over a road full of potholes. If you focus on steering, braking and eyeing the road, you'll come out safely.

This is also a time for thinking creatively. Shift your perspective and start seeing the glass "half full" instead of "half empty." Set your mind free to dream and imagine a myriad of happy endings.

Find some quiet time to be alone, relax and think. Get your old job (and whatever bothered you) out of your system so you can move on. Focus on what you value most and how you can get it. Keep a journal. Record your thoughts and experiences. Writing gives voice to your unconscious and is cathartic as well.

New Beginnings

Imagine yourself emerging from a forest. You're lost, bewildered, and confused. Suddenly, you see the road to your destination right in front of you! Now you have your bearings. You're comfortable, less stressed, more focused. *So, when does all this happen?*—you ask. Bridges says that the timing is up to you.

- You left your old job and accept that it's behind you.
- You gave yourself solitude and peace.
- You spent time in your Neutral Zone, exploring challenges and dreams.
- You embarked on a journey toward a new sense of purpose.
- Something tells you it's time to act.

Now it is important that your idea for a New Beginning holds up under scrutiny.

Purpose. Ask yourself, "Why am I doing this?" Be clear and be able to communicate both the question and the answers articulately.

Picture. How does your New Beginning look and feel? Use your imagination, your senses, pictures, music...

> *They say time changes things, but you actually have to change them yourself.*
>
> Andy Warhol

Plan. How will your New Beginning evolve from point A to point B? What are your alternative plans in case glitches occur? What are the most reasonable time frames you can construct?

Part. What's your part in all this, and how do others play supporting roles?

Now, you must shift your focus away from the result and get down to the nitty-gritty. Take small steps—everyday —to arrive at your destination.

You've been away from the job market for some time and you want to get back

You're back on the market. You suddenly realize things have changed. Your experience is no longer current. Your skills are outdated. The longer you've been away from the workforce, the more challenging the task of finding a fit. You need to assess your marketability based on your current skills and knowledge and define a course of action. The critical objective is to identify a direction that will enable you to re-enter the workforce and be happy.

Separate feelings from actions

"They're not recognizing the true value I bring to the table." "They're concerned over the time I'll miss because my children are in school." "They're not confident that I'm committed for the long haul." "They're afraid I might not fit in with the younger crowd." "They're not saying so, but they think I'm a bit out of date." These thoughts are the mental confidence bashers that are counterproductive to finding employment. Don't become a victim of your own lack of confidence.

> *We cannot become what we need to be by remaining what we are.*
>
> Max Depree

Your task is to convince the employer that you have something unique to offer—perhaps your a superb communicator, a skilled negotiator, perhaps your work ethic is second to none or you're an excellent project manager. In fact, you're skills may not be out of date at all. Maybe you haven't been away from work for that long. But if your skills are indeed out of date, then go update them. Regardless, get out there and promote your virtues, emphasize your comparative advantage, and make them want you.

Study the market, determine the going rate for individuals with your skill set. Then demonstrate how your value exceeds your price.

Recognize your emotions

Yes, your confidence has been eroded. You have difficulty accepting the fact that employers do not recognize the value you bring to the table. And yes, you have a fear that a lot has changed since you last worked.

You will experience a number of emotions when you attempt to re-enter the job market. Recognize them, and put them in perspective. This is important because most of these feelings will erode your confidence when you need it most.

> *There is no failure except in no longer trying.*
> Elbert Hubbard

Apprehensive? You have a right to feel apprehensive. You have a concern that you may not be competitive. Go ahead, talk to your biggest boosters—your best friend, your significant other, a sibling.

Disappointed? You're upset that employers do not appreciate your value. You feel like a failure. You regret that you took time off. Go ahead, review your achievements and successes. Write a testimonial to yourself. You'll discover there's a lot more there than you first thought.

Angry? Be mad. You've put in a lot of time. You have a right to be recognized. Don't internalize the anger. Go ahead, go to the gym, walk around the block, play a round of golf.

Self-doubt? You're doubting your ability to perform. Go ahead, review your accomplishments. Write them down. You've been successful before, you will succeed again.

Inadequate? You're concerned you don't have the skills and competencies to compete in today's marketplace. Go ahead, talk to a career counselor (local colleges, YMCA or recommended professional). Validate that your chosen career direction is correct. Determine what course of action will fill any gaps in your skill set.

> *Don't find fault, find a remedy.*
> Henry Ford

Maintain a balance

Don't wallow in self-doubt. Recognize your concerns and put them in perspective. You have strengths and attributes that make you marketable. If you need to upgrade your skills get on with the task. To get a job you need to identify and recognize your disadvantages and take affirmative action. Shout out your strengths and capabilities. Give employers compelling reasons to hire you.

You recently arrived from another country and need employment

Your move has not been an easy one. You left friends, relatives, a job and familiarity behind. You're in a new country and you need to adapt to the culture. Most important, you need to find a job. Recognize that you are going to face barriers finding equivalent employment in your field. To succeed you need to develop a plan to stay on course. It won't be easy but you will get there.

Separate feelings from actions

"They're not recognizing my qualifications." "I've spent years in my field and it means nothing to them." "I was a respected professional in my country and all I can get here is a low-skilled position." "I've stepped back 10 years and now I have to start at the bottom." "I didn't realize the challenges I would face finding suitable employment before I moved here."

> *If you can dream it, you can do it. Always remember that this whole thing was started with a dream and a mouse.*
>
> Walt Disney

Alright, you're at a disadvantage. The rules of the game may be skewed against you but, the reality is, you need to find a viable career opportunity that capitalizes on your skills and experiences. You need to take positive and affirmative action. You may be able to re-qualify within your profession or pursue a parallel opportunity within your field that may not have the same stringent requirements.

Recognize your emotions

Your pride has been injured and your anger is fueled. You are going to experience a number of emotions. Deal with them in order to avoid the anger that will undermine the quest toward your best opportunity.

> **You must do the things you cannot do.**
> *Eleanor Roosevelt*

Disillusioned? You expected more. Your dream is shattered. Reality is cruel. Go ahead, talk to a previous newcomer who has pursued a successful career. Identify people within your community who will understand the challenges you face and who will offer support.

Cheated? You were led to believe that the streets were paved with gold. You can't get the job you want and the alternatives are unattractive. You feel invalidated. Go ahead and be angry. Revisit your options and place them in proper perspective. You may have to accept a less attractive position as an interim step.

Hopeless? You don't see a way out. You feel trapped. You feel inconsequential. Go ahead, seek the assistance of a psychologist or professional who will help you confront this debilitating emotion. He or she will also enable you to examine your goals, ensuring that you set realistic and attainable expectations, both short-term and longer-term.

Maintain a balance

Anger is debilitating when you're in job search mode. Re-examine your goals and ensure they are realistic. Treat the short-term solution as a step on the way toward your desired long-term goal.

> **If you don't like something, change it; if you can't change it, change the way you think about it.**
> *Mary Engelbreit*

Tenacity and a positive approach are keys to success in obtaining a satisfactory position that will meet your needs. Ingenuity is another strategy that will enable you to break down barriers. For example, you may offer to undertake gratis a special project for a prospective employer, or you may accept a short-term contract to demonstrate your capability.

You recently graduated and find that employers want experience

You've spent four grueling post-high-school years pursuing an education and anticipated a good job as the reward on graduation. Your grades are excellent, yet you're having difficulty landing an acceptable position. You're in a Catch-22: without the experience you can't get the right job; without the right job you can't get the experience. You need to develop a plan that will get you out of the loop and to the next level, a plan that will likely involve interim steps.

Separate feelings from actions

"My education means nothing to them." "They want me to start at the bottom." "Experience, not education, is what they're really after." "They seem unwilling to take me on as an intern and let me earn my stripes." "They're telling me that my expectations are too high." These are some of the thoughts you'll come away with when you look for work. But don't let the job search process rob you of your spirit and drive. You need to be tenacious to succeed. Set realistic goals. Put in place a strategy that will set you on the right course to your desired position.

Recognize your emotions

It's not easy trying to get your first post-university or post-college job. You know you hold qualifications that the market values. Yet market conditions run hot and cold which can make entry difficult. And it needs to be remembered that you are not alone out there. There are others competing for the same job and some of these competitors have experience to boot. So, you need to keep a cool head. Plan your strategy and execute your plan carefully. Do not let rejection and adversity get you down. You must remain positive to succeed.

Discouraged? You spent four years in post-secondary education and can't get a job. Opportunities for graduates in your field have dried up. Go ahead, vent your disappointment. Talk about your concerns with friends and relatives. Seek solace in the knowledge that you will find a satisfactory solution. Timing and realistic goals are key.

> *Prosperity tries the fortunate, adversity the great.*
>
> Rose F. Kennedy

Misled? You worked hard qualifying for a position in your chosen field and after years of preparation you find the pickings slim. Not everyone within the graduating class will find his/her intended job. Go ahead, vent your disapproval. Write your elected representative. Talk to executives in organizations that would have been on your target list. Determine if the current scenario is structural and long-term or market driven and subject to change. If market driven, when might a positive change be expected? Entry just down the road may be possible. Regardless, you need to focus on applying your capabilities to the market and aligning your skills with opportunities.

Flustered? You're feeling upset. You're not sure what steps to take next. You're feeling alone and quite marginalized. Go ahead, talk to a good friend, someone you can confide in who sees the positive in situations. You need to control your frustration, get the anger behind you, devise a strategy and work it.

Maintain a balance

You need to assess your marketability based on market opportunity and ensure your skills are appropriate to the position you seek. You need to define a course of action that will enable you to migrate toward the desired position by acquiring the necessary experience. You need to move forward in manageable steps. Securing your first position may require some sacrifice in pride. Recognize that your focus must be on the short-term steps required to reach the longer-term goal. Your competitive advantage may be in accepting a lesser position than originally expected in order to get your foot in the door. Ask yourself: how many senior executives started their careers in the mail room or on the warehouse floor?

> **Success isn't purchased at any one time, but on the installment plan.**
>
> *Anonymous*

Take extreme care of yourself

You're stressed out and that's understandable. All your thoughts are focused on not having a job! Stop. Don't allow stress, fear and anxiety to overtake you and rob you of the physical strength and spirit you need to find the job that's waiting.

Eat well. Give yourself regular, nourishing, healthy meals. Consider taking a vitamin supplement. Lay off the junk food, alcohol and drugs.

Exercise. It's proven to reduce stress and ward off depression.

Have some fun. Get back into your hobbies. They'll help you reconnect with your inner self.

> *Who bothers to cook TV dinners? I suck them frozen.*
> Woody Allen

Laugh. It releases chemicals in the brain that help the mind and body.

Renew your spirit. If you have faith in a higher power, make time to meditate or attend services. Studies have shown that spiritual activities can relieve stress and help you focus on a positive target.

Volunteer. Get outside of yourself. Let someone else be the center of attention for an hour. Your problems may seem insurmountable, but many people would kill to wake up in your body.

Reach out to family

You're not alone in this. Your family will experience anxiety and fear along with you. Don't shut them out or tell them little white lies about your prospects. Practice openness and be supportive.

Be up front. Tell them that you're in job search mode and under duress and looking for a new opportunity. Steer the conversation to the future. Allow them to give you emotional support. Then give it back to them.

Talk. Tell them about your action plans and how you'll be spending your time. Don't lead them on or disappoint them by making promises about landing a job right away. It takes time, often 3 to 6 months. Your job, for the present, is to find a job.

> *Reality check: it may take 3 to 6 months to find your next job.*

Listen. They'll have, understandably, worries and concerns. They'll also have valuable suggestions.

Encourage family unity. You're at home now, so make the most of it. Get involved in day-to-day activities. Cook. Spruce up the house. Help with homework. Plan family evenings. Your good vibes will have a calming effect on everyone.

Coach the curious

Without trying, your family can push your buttons in all the wrong ways. Tell them you welcome their input, but are particularly sensitive at this time. Ask them to refrain from killer phrases that are hurtful and non-constructive. Whether you are in job search mode as a result of downsizing or are job searching for other reasons, some of the worst offenders such as those below may be present in your own home.

> *Confidence is contagious. So is lack of confidence.*
> Vince Lombardi

Here are the *Top 10 Things Not to Say to Your Unemployed Spouse*:

1. **"What did you do today?"** This will extinguish conversation and may create anxiety. Instead, set aside a specific time each week to discuss the job search in a positive and proactive manner.

2. **"How long is it going to take to find a job?"** Your spouse can't answer that because he or she can't predict the future. Unemployment creates a feeling of powerlessness. To re-establish control, encourage your spouse to establish a daily routine. Create a written re-employment plan and work that plan daily.

3. **"We really can't afford that."** This is a natural reaction and may be true. It is important to insure that your spouse or significant other is a full fiscal partner throughout the re-employment process. Look at your family's income and expenses together, and access your financial picture realistically and proactively.

4. **"If only you had . . ."** The emotion of regret can be excruciating and overwhelming. It is important to understand the emotional wave that unemployment creates. These emo-

tions include Shock and Denial, Fear and Panic, Anger, Bargaining and Temporary Acceptance. Regret is a natural by-product of job loss. Understand job-loss grief and manage through the process without directing blame at you or your spouse.

5. **"This is all your fault."** In most cases, there is nothing your spouse could have done to change or influence the downsizing or layoff. Communication as a family is critical. Blame is not constructive, won't change the outcome and only makes a very difficult situation worse.

6. **"We will never recover from this."** Because your family's livelihood has been eliminated, it is appropriate to feel a tremendous sense of violation and fear. Uncontrolled fear can quickly immobilize both your spouse and family unit. The key to reducing fear is to put your concerns into perspective. Create a "worry time" each day and restrict worrying to that time slot. When worry threatens to overwhelm, make an "appointment" to deal with it only at the appointed time.

> *Worry does not empty tomorrow of its sorrow. It empties today of its strength.*
> Corrie ten Boom

7. **"What did you really do that got you downsized?"** In many cases layoff decisions are decided by upper management, made without your spouse's consent, and handed down from the top. It is important to focus on the future that you can change and accept the past that cannot be changed.

8. **"We have no choice."** Life requires all of us to make daily choices. All appear to be right at the time, but sometimes they are not. Hindsight is always 20/20, and painful mistakes are often made. However, dwelling on past decisions will not change the future. Instead, focus on the re-employment process, and take it one day at a time.

9. **"I can't stand this any longer."** The hardest part of unemployment is the not knowing when it will end.

Frustration is a continuous part of the re-employment process, but it is important to strive to maintain as much normality in your home life as possible. Realize that you can't look for a job 24 hours a day, seven days a week. Encourage your spouse to leave the job hunt behind at the end of the day and make time to be a parent, spouse and part of the family.

10. **"What happened to all of your friends ... You know the ones who said they would have a job for you if you ever needed one?"** Most have found that the friends that they thought would help them the most usually help them the least, and complete strangers out of the generosity of their heart bend over backwards to help. Unemployment is a temporary condition, not a disease.

The above list is reprinted with permission of J. Damian Birkel, author of *Career Bounce-Back!, Surfing the Emotional Wave* and founder of Professionals in Transition Support Group Inc. (www.jobsearching.org), one of the oldest non-profit job-searching support groups in America

Tune in to kids' stuff

Children can be profoundly affected by job transition, and often don't know how to articulate their feelings. They often "act out" their fear, confusion and anxieties. So don't overburden them with emotional or financial details that are beyond their grasp. Alert their teachers to your situation and be aware of behavioral problems before they become serious.

Open the lines of communication. Keep kids in the loop. They have a way of writing their own scripts which contain the worst possible endings. Protect them from their own irrational fears.

Make sure they know it's no one's fault. Kids may harbor a mistaken belief that you did something wrong. Or they may think they're responsible and have become a financial burden. Reassure them, regardless of their age.

> *I will not pop corn while Dad is on the phone.*
>
> Bart Simpson

Let them help. Involve kids in the process by giving them responsibilities. Can they do more around the house? Show you their favorite Web search engines? Curb their spending? Get an after-school job?

Activate your stress busters

As soon as you start to feel yourself spiraling downward into anxiety, nip it in the bud. Stress and worry can crush you and slow down the process of finding a job. When you change your thoughts you'll change events. Here are some suggestions:

Write down your stressors. When you can locate and name your triggers, you gain control over them. A stressor may involve seeing other people dressed and going to work. It could be watching TV where everyone seems to have a glamorous job. Or it might be the letter carrier's arrival because you dread the bills. Be aware of the signals that send you off into stress mode. List them. Challenge them. Avoid them. If they include social or financial obligations, look for ways to lessen or postpone them.

> *Nothing in life is to be feared, it is only to be understood.*
>
> Marie Curie

Establish your priorities. Don't let your time be siphoned off by activities that are not related to your job search. Set a daily routine and stick to it. Allow time for family and relaxation. But your first order of business is to conduct an effective search that gets you working again soon.

Complete tasks. You'll gain a sense of accomplishment if you perform small tasks each day. Scan the newspapers. Mine the vast resources on the Internet. Organize stationery for resumés you'll mail. Get a haircut. Get off your butt. Get the idea?

Pay attention to your breathing. If it's short and shallow, sit quietly with your eyes closed. Take 10 deep breaths. Concentrate on the air going in and out of your lungs. Gently push away any other thoughts that come into your mind. Do this often to refocus and regain composure.

Music soothes the savage breast. It has the ability to shift you into a gentler headspace in minutes. Try meditation tapes too, available at your library.

Avoid isolation. Do not allow yourself to become alienated from colleagues, friends, neighbors and family because you think there's a stigma attached to being out of work. Many will have inspirational stories of their own.

> *One of the symptoms of an approaching nervous breakdown is the belief that one's work is terribly important.*
>
> Bertrand Russell

Take personal inventory

Right now, you're worried sick about finding a job. *Stop!* These thoughts are clogging your mind and preventing you from thinking constructively about controlling your change. Replace these thoughts with a review of your most worthwhile characteristics.

List your achievements. You've had more success than failure, so focus on the good. A friend who knows you well will be able to help. Keep this list for updating your resumé and speaking about yourself in interviews.

Remind yourself continually. Tape your list of achievements to the bathroom mirror. Replay it mentally. Strengthen your connection to your success. Keep your achievements top-of-mind so there's no room for self-defeating recriminations.

> *What lies behind us and what lies before us are tiny matters compared to what lies within us.*
>
> Ralph Waldo Emerson

Reward yourself. You've already done a great deal in your life and you're gearing up to do more. You deserve candles with dinner, a good book and a cushy chair, a relaxing bath and facial. No? Not your style? Then how about a sweaty game of pick-up hockey, extreme Frisbee with the dog, or a weekend of action videos? Name your catharsis. But be cautious with alcohol. It interferes with sleep and acts as a depressant.

Know your weaknesses. You may have areas that need personal development. Now's the time to read up or take courses on interpersonal skills, computer programs or dressing for success. These are not character flaws, just gaps that need to be addressed.

Use realistic yardsticks. Avoid measuring yourself against impossible standards. You're not Albert Einstein, Bill Gates or Martha Stewart. Judge yourself *only* against yourself. You're at a certain point in your journey, with a new road ahead. How far have you come? How far do you want to go?

Picture success. Top athletes often visualize themselves winning the game. This gives them the confidence they need to follow through and make it happen. Borrow this technique and get yourself into the zone. Picture yourself living your New Beginning. Behave as if it's already happening.

> *No one can make you feel inferior without your consent.*
> Eleanor Roosevelt

Start fresh

How many times has something unexpected come into your life and changed it for the better? A new relationship, a chance to travel, an inheritance or gift? You did not seek these things, yet you were dealt a lucky hand. You were given a fresh start.

In job search, you have another opportunity for a fresh start. You may not see this as a gift, since you're not sure how things will turn out. But you're in a unique position to take control of your life, chart your path and find fulfillment. Embrace your good fortune.

> *When one door closes, another door opens. But we look so long at the closed door, we don't see the ones that open for us.*
>
> Alexander Graham Bell

Live in the present. The past is history and you cannot change it. Yes, you may have lost or been squeezed out of your last job. But don't play your misery tapes over and over again. *Let go of the past.* Let it slip gently into history. Stop wanting what you've lost. Put it all behind you and take only what you've learned.

Take responsibility for your actions. You may have made mistakes. Who hasn't? Even the most successful business people make colossal errors. But they don't spend their lives wringing their hands over it. They simply start again, with new knowledge, and grab hold of the next opportunity. Avoid heavy-duty guilt trips. Make your corrections and step forward.

Quit blaming. Don't waste time and energy complaining, gossiping or blaming old villains. Conserve your energy. You need it to create your next adventure. Remember what George Herbert said: "Living well is the best revenge."

Remain calm. "God, grant me the serenity to accept the things I cannot change, the courage to change the things I can, and the wisdom to know the difference." (*The Serenity Prayer*)

Take command and enlist others. You are the captain of your ship and headed for your New World. Chart your destination but be prepared for storms. Rally your resource or support team—family members, friends, clergy and professional acquaintances—who can help you stay on course. Take advantage of their moral, medical, emotional and financial support.

Express yourself. Don't bottle up your emotions. Vent! That's what friends and coaches are for. Get those lemons out on the table and squeeze some lemonade.

Name your fears. Look the enemy square in the face and give it a name. Is it Failure? Homelessness? Divorce? Loneliness? Bankruptcy? Write it on a piece of paper. Make it real so you can recognize it and gain the upper hand. Put that paper in an envelope and stash it on a shelf, out of the way, where it belongs.

Be a crocodile. Develop a thick skin and never take rejection personally. You'll go through many interviews before getting the offer that's right for you. If people have pointers, take what you think is valuable and use it.

Take risks. Circumstances may prevent you from getting your dream job. Keep in mind that you have a great deal to offer and so does the world. Have a Plan B. Take a gamble on something new if it's offered. You may find that it's ideal after all. How many times have you heard: "Getting fired was the best thing that ever happened to me?"

> *You'll always miss 100% of the shots you never take.*
> Wayne Gretzky

Get into a group. Support groups work because they bring together people who are experiencing similar circumstances. A group will give you a safe place to talk, sympathy and understanding, companionship, a network, and actionable ideas.

Get into a groove

It's easy to feel sorry for yourself thinking that the worst is

still to come. Chances are, the worst has already happened. And guess what? You're still here. So stay busy with the job of finding a job, and there'll be no time for pity parties.

Resist the temptation to sleep late and watch TV. It anesthetizes and impedes your progress. You can shorten your job search by setting up a routine and sticking to it.

Get up every day as if you were going to work, because you are working—working on a major transition. Dig out your daytimer and make appointments with yourself and others. Keep them.

Here's an example:

Tuesday, April 17

8:00 a.m.	Make pancakes for the kids
9:00	Read the papers and check want ads. Make note of companies in the news.
10:00	Explore company Web sites for job postings
11:00	Work on updating resumé
12:00 p.m.	Exercise, do household chores
1:00	Lunch with a friend
2:00	Shop, pick up relevant materials at the library
3:00	Get on the phone to network and follow up

4:00	Pick up kids and take them to hockey practice. Yell a little.
5:00	Focus. Meditate. Visualize goals. Allow ideas to surface. Read.
6:00	Have a simple dinner with family. Give them an update.
7:00	Shower, relax. Spend time with spouse.
8:00	Meet with support group
9:00	Free time
10:00	Watch the news, do laundry or other chores
11:00	Set alarm and get a good night's rest

Have an interim financial plan

Financial experts recommend having enough savings to last six months in case of emergencies. But your savings may be far more modest. So if job loss was sudden and unexpected, and if things are tight, you should take immediate action to review your expenses and resources.

> **Gentlemen prefer bonds.**
> *Andrew Mellon*

At this time you may have little or no income. It's important to cover your basic expenses and curtail the extras. Enroll your family in the process, since they'll directly impact on your bills. They might even be motivated to earn their own money for things that aren't on the menu right now.

Apply for unemployment insurance benefits immediately. You'll need a record of employment from your employer. If you qualify, you'll receive substantially less than your previous salary. If you received severance, it will reduce your entitlement. Current legislation lengthens the time it takes before your first check arrives. It shortens the number of weeks you can draw benefits.

Investigate Federal/State/Provincial employment support programs. Depending on your income and employment situation—students, newcomers, back-to-work parents, the disabled—the availability of financial support programs for employers and individuals is worth investigating.

Review your health coverage. If your partner is covered at work, she or he may be able to switch to a family plan. If you belong to a professional organization, or are an alumnus of a college or university, you may be able to get group coverage. Or you may decide that your existing health care coverage is sufficient for the time being.

Talk to a professional. A bank manager or financial professional will have ideas to help you get through this period. You may be able to borrow against your house or life insurance policies. He or she will help you get your financial house in order.

Take stock of your assets. You will probably have to dip into savings accounts, investment and retirement savings plans. You may also have to use a line of credit, if you have one. If you're lucky, you'll have received a severance package, or your spouse is making enough to get you by for the time being. These are all pieces of the financial puzzle you must pull together *now*.

> *Live like a millionaire: below your means.*

Make a detailed budget and live by it. List your household expenses. Figure out what you need every month *just for the essentials*. Live frugally. Ask yourself if you really need the cell phone, cable TV, costly restaurant meals and entertainment, new clothes, trips and so on.

Save your receipts. You may be eligible for income tax deductions for legal fees, tax preparation, relocation costs and moving expenses.

Fill in your financial worksheets

Assess at regular intervals and adjust your spending where and when necessary. Your liquid assets will be accessible more quickly and easily in a crunch. In order of accessibility, this would include cash on hand, cash and equivalent amounts in banks or financial institutions—checking and savings accounts and money market funds, short-term certificates of deposit and cash value of whole life insurance.

Fixed-rate assets—government bonds, corporate bonds and municipal bonds—fluctuate in realizable value with money market conditions but are readily convertible into cash. Your equity assets—stocks and mutual funds—can be sold, but dollar amounts realized are subject to financial market conditions. Keep an eye on investments in fixed-principal assets maturing in the short term.

Your equity in tangible assets such as art, jewelry, furnishings and automobiles may be liquidated, if required. And equity in vacation property, investment property, and your primary residence may also be liquidated, if necessary.

Know where you stand financially in order to make correct personal funding decisions, especially under conditions of duress. Assess and know your net worth on an ongoing basis—the value of your assets (what you own) less the value of your liabilities (what you owe). And, maintain a monthly budget showing sources of income and expenses.

Financial templates and calculators can be found on many banking institution Web sites or by entering "personal net worth" or "financial calculator" in your favorite Internet search engine. Key in "personal budgeting" to find budgeting tips and worksheets to help manage your monthly personal expenses. Choose the format that best meets your needs. Engage your bank manager or a financial professional especially if asset restructuring or borrowing is on the horizon.

Personal net worth statement

ASSETS:

Cash & cash equivalents:
Cash on hand
Checking accounts
Savings accounts
Short-term certificates
of deposit
Cash value of whole life
insurance
Other cash accounts

Fixed-rate assets:
Government bonds
Municipal bonds
Corporate bonds
Other fixed-rate assets

Fixed-principal assets:
Term deposits
Fixed-dollar annuities
Other fixed-principal assets

Equity assets:
Stocks
Variable annuities
Retirement plans
Limited partnerships
Business interests
Other equity assets

Tangible assets:
   Primary residence
   Vacation home
   Investment property
   Furnishings
   Automobiles
   Art, jewelry and other
      valuables
   Other tangible assets

Total dollar value of assets:

LIABILITIES:

Mortgage on primary
   residence
Other mortgages
Automobile loans
Bank loans
Personal loans
Credit card debt
Other debts

Total dollar value of liabilities:

Net worth:
(dollar value of assets less dollar value of liabilities)

Record date of estimate:

Personal budget

Monthly Income:

Wages
Bonuses
Commissions
Severance pay
Unemployment insurance
Interest income
Capital gains income
Dividend income
Other income

Total Monthly Income:

Monthly Expenses:

Food & personal care items:
Groceries
Household consumables
Eating out
Other food & personal care items

Housing:
Mortgage or rent
Property tax
Home insurance
Gas
Water
Electricity
Waste removal
Telephone
Internet access
Cable TV

Home repairs

Maintenance

Other household expenses

Clothing:

Personal wear items

Family needs

Dry cleaning

Other clothing expenses

Transportation:

Car payments

Gasoline and oil

Parking

Automobile repairs

License, permits and other fees

Other transportation costs (tolls, bus, subway, etc.)

Medical:

Prescriptions

Over-the-counter drugs

Medical care

Dental care

Vision care

Health insurance

Other medical expenses

Personal:

Life insurance

Disability insurance

Professional dues

Other personal expenses

Financial Charges:

Interest on credit cards

State/provincial income tax

Federal income tax

Other loans and financial charges

Miscellaneous expenses:

Entertainment

Travel

Magazine and newspaper subscriptions

Pet care

Hobbies

Gifts

Charitable donations

Alimony

Care for adult dependant

Other expenses

Total Monthly Expenses:

Note: Prorate bi-monthly, quarterly and semi-annual expenses
to a monthly dollar amount.

Get a grip on unnecessary expenses

If you're like most people who suddenly find themselves in job search mode, your expenses during this period will be far greater than your income. So reduce your expenses and control your household spending. Be firm with your family.

> **Even though work stops, expenses run on.**
> *Cato the Elder*

Use credit cards wisely. Interest charges could build to a point where you'll pay double for an item you bought on sale. Department store cards can charge double-digit rates. If you need a card for emergencies, switch to a low-interest, no-frills card at your bank. Interest is significantly lower. Pay your minimums each month and maintain your good credit.

Contact your mortgage holder and investigate renegotiating your terms and/or delaying your payments.

Sell luxury items you don't really need such as second cars, boats, laptop computers and other expensive toys. You'll also save on the associated insurance and maintenance costs.

Shop for better rates when your insurance comes up for renewal. You can save by "bundling" all your policies with one insurer. There are discounts for drivers and homeowners over 50, so ask. Also, you can reduce your premiums by increasing your deductibles, but again, you have to ask. Get an independent insurance broker working on your behalf.

Repair rather than replace big-ticket items such as refrigerators, stoves, dishwashers and freezers.

Conserve heat and energy. Adjust the thermostat. Wash only full loads of dishes and clothes. Conserve gasoline by making one trip instead of several. Search the Web for sites dedicated to frugal living. There are plenty of tips that can save you thousands of dollars in unnecessary expenses.

Eat in instead of out. There's nothing faster, healthier or cheaper than inventing your own meals. The kitchen has always been a natural meeting place for family and friends, so grab a goofy apron and become a magnet for fun, relaxation and camaraderie. You'll save money and reduce stress.

> *Beware of little expenses. A small leak will sink a great ship.*
> Benjamin Franklin

Want what you have, and you'll have what you want. It's the secret of feeling abundantly satisfied.

These are things I'm doing for myself

- Learning to separate my feelings from my actions.
- Recognizing and affirming my emotions.
- Working through the grief process where job search involves job loss.
- Understanding my Endings, Neutral Zones and New Beginnings.
- Taking extreme care of myself.
- Reaching out to family.
- Coaching the curious.
- Tuning in to my kids.
- Writing things down in a special transition journal.
- Taking personal inventory.
- Identifying with my successes.
- Activating my stress busters.
- Keeping a daily appointment diary.
- Maintaining a routine.
- Establishing an interim financial plan.

> *I've got my faults, but living in the past isn't one of them. There's no future in it.*
>
> Sparky Anderson

STEP 2:
Find Your Best Fit

In Step 1, you faced your fears and resolved to make this transition a positive one. You set up your support network and enrolled your family in the process. You established a daily routine and a financial plan.

Now it's time to take an objective look at your current skill set, and see how it fits with today's job market.

> *Ride the horse in the direction it's going.*
>
> Werner Erhard

Be realistic and pragmatic. There's no sense dreaming about an ideal job if your qualifications don't dovetail with the requirements. It's also foolish to overlook opportunities that exist if you're willing to transfer your skills to new areas. Be open-minded and flexible.

Change is inevitable, except in vending machines

In the 1950s and 60s, people expected to work at the same job their entire working careers, then receive a gold watch and pension at retirement. Today, fewer people receive company pensions and even fewer work at one career their entire lives. Retirement itself may become an outdated concept as we live longer and switch to part-time work in later years.

Globalization and technological advances have brought monumental changes in the ways companies do business and the ways employees move from job to job. Adaptability is key, and lifelong learners who constantly upgrade their skills have the best chance of surviving and succeeding.

> *The pine that bends with the wind survives the winter.*
> *Oriental proverb*

Just like any other market, the job market functions on supply and demand. If you have the skills that are needed, you'll find work easily. If you don't, it's time to make yourself more marketable.

Get out your notebook. Write down your answers to these questions. Take your time. You'll make important discoveries.

- What kind of a lifestyle do I want at this point in my life?
- Am I willing to switch to a new career that allows for that lifestyle?
- Am I willing to work for less money but for more personal freedom and fulfillment?
- What are the current opportunities for someone with my skill set?
- Which industries are growing and which are flat or in decline?
- What are the gaps between my skills and what the market wants?
- How can I close these gaps?

Understand your place in history

Your attitudes about work have been shaped by your generation. If you've experienced personality conflicts in the workplace, they may be traceable to unspoken ideas that each generation has regarding our jobs and their meanings. Here are a few insights from *Generations at Work* by Zemke, Raines and Filipczak that will help you better understand how each generation looks at work.

> *Your neighbor's vision is as true for him as your own vision is true for you.*
> Miguel de Unamuno

VETERANS.

Born between 1922 and 1943. They value dedication and sacrifice, hard work and conformity. They are patient and respect authority. They put duty before pleasure and have a sense of honor. Their heroes include Superman, Winston Churchill, Babe Ruth and Joe DiMaggio.

Veteran Attributes. Veterans are loyal, stable, detail-oriented, thorough and hard working. However, younger workers say they cannot handle ambiguity or change, are reluctant to buck the system, are uncomfortable with conflict and don't speak up when they disagree.

BABY BOOMERS.

Born between 1943 and 1960. They represent one third of the population in North America so chances are, you'll find yourself working with a Boomer. They're characterized by optimism, team spirit, a desire for personal gratification, an interest in health, well-being and personal growth. And they like to be involved. Their heroes include Gandhi, Martin Luther King and John Glenn.

Baby Boomer Attributes. Boomers are driven, service-oriented individuals who are willing to go the extra mile. They value good working relationships and are team players. However, non-Boomers may find them cavalier about budgets, reluctant to go against their peers, too focused on the process rather than the result, overly sensitive to feedback, self-centered and judgmental of those who see things differently.

GENERATION X.

Born between 1960 and 1980. Gen Xers don't have any heroes and this speaks volumes about them. However, they value diversity, global thinking, balance, technological literacy, informality and fun, self-reliance and pragmatism.

> *It's not easy being green.*
> Kermit the Frog

Gen Xer Attributes. Gen Xers are adaptable techno-wizards who are independent, creative and unintimidated by authority. However, older employees may find them impatient, lacking people skills, inexperienced and cynical.

GENERATION NEXT.

Born between 1980 and 2000. Nexters have a sense of civic duty, optimism, morality and confidence. They are achievement-oriented individuals who are sociable and comfortable with diversity. They also have plenty of street smarts. Their heroes include Tiger Woods, Christopher Reeve, Princess Diana, Bill Gates and Mother Teresa.

Nexter Attributes. Nexters can brag about being technologically savvy, optimistic, tenacious, capable of multitasking and collective action. But older workers say Nexters need a great deal of structure and supervision. They're also inexperienced handling difficult "people issues."

Know thyself:
a skills inventory

While you were working, you may not have paid much attention to the skills you were acquiring and building. Carefully think back. Write a detailed list of the skills required to do *each job* you held. Write down *everything* you can think of. Here are some examples and thought starters. Your particular profession may be completely different. But your list of skills will be equally extensive and impressive.

MARKETING / SALES / CUSTOMER SERVICE

Marketing of products
and services
Market research and analysis
Competitive analysis
Product / Brand management
Category management
Business development
Advertising, promotion,
public relations
Buying
Customer service
Fundraising
Community relations

DESIGN / WRITING

Strategic and creative
development
Marketing materials
Advertising campaigns in
TV, print, radio
Promotions / Events planning
and execution
Web site design and
content provision
Collateral / Catalogs
Specialized writing

MANAGEMENT / ADMINISTRATION

Directed a Management Team
Approved corporate objectives
Approved business plans
Approved budgets
Reported to Board of Directors
Ensured effectiveness and
efficiency of business processes
Contributed to organizational
planning
Built teams
Conducted performance reviews
Solved problems
Provided strategic analysis
Project management
Union negotiations
Regulatory reporting
Licensing, purchasing, pricing,
scheduling
Communications

INFORMATION SYSTEMS

Information systems
management
Information systems architecture
Requirements analysis

Systems development
Business systems analysis
  and planning
Data center operation
Telecommunication networks
Network analysis
Voice and data carriers
Hardware technology
Distributed processing
Programming
Systems design
Database design
Performance monitoring
Diagnostics
Software technology
Software analysis
Software development
Web development
Web design, graphics and text
Office automation
Timesharing

OPERATIONS

Research and development
Production
Budget planning
Expense management
Efficiency monitoring
Manufacturing
Process engineering
Systems development
Project management
Construction
Financial management
Materials management
Administration
Production management
Quality control
Purchasing
Customer service
Warehousing

Logistics
Retail chain management
Retail district management
Store management

RESEARCH / ENGINEERING

Research and development
New product development
Plant design and construction
Process engineering
Process development
Field applied research
Diagnostics
Synthesizing
Licensing
Patent strategy

HUMAN RESOURCES

Recruiting
Training and development
Organizational development
Career development
Performance evaluation
Staff planning and analysis
Compensation and benefits
Health and safety
Wage and salary administration
Policy and procedures planning
Employee relations
Labor relations
Collective bargaining

SUPPORT PROFESSIONS

Reception
Administrative support
Courier
Executive support
Data entry

FINANCE / ACCOUNTING
Strategic planning
Financial planning
Capital budgeting
Audit
Forensic accounting
Management reporting
Planning and analysis
Standard controls
General accounting
Cost accounting
Internal controls
Forecasting
Price modeling
Inventory control
Treasury
Credit
Cash management
Debt negotiations
Domestic tax
International tax
New business development
Foreign exchange
Financial data processing
Business valuation
Mergers and acquisitions
Risk management
Actuarial analysis

SKILLED TRADES
Carpentry
Electrical
Masonry
Drywall
Printing
Cooking
Landscaping
Plumbing
Building maintenance
Heating, ventilation,
   air conditioning maintenance
Machinery
Tool & die making

PEOPLE PROFESSIONS
Social work
Childcare
Care of the elderly
Counseling
Fundraising
Funeral directing
Psychology

HEALTH PROFESSIONS
Pharmacy
Nursing
Medicine
Dentistry
Medical imaging
Naturopathy
Veterinary science
Chiropractic
Chiropody
Podiatry

ACADEMIC
Teaching and training
Curriculum design
Research
Tutoring
Special needs education

List your accomplishments

At this point, you have a long list of skills you've developed. Now you'll list your accomplishments—the unique selling points that will distinguish you on your resumé and at interviews.

Your accomplishments are different than your skills. Accomplishments are *actual milestones* you achieved throughout your career. Perhaps you increased sales, streamlined a work process, launched a new product, developed a Web site or won an award. In the process, you may have improved organizational effectiveness, introduced new technologies or enhanced the company's image.

> **Hey Rocky, watch me pull a rabbit out of my hat!**
> *Bullwinkle Moose*

Now, make a list of the companies you worked for over your career. Write a detailed account of your *accomplishments*, by company and by position. Don't be shy. Lay claim to your achievements. Champion your milestones. Quantify these results wherever you can. This activity is a critical step in the development of an effective resumé.

Write your list using action verbs such as "directed," "engineered," "spearheaded," "created," and "improved." Need more? There's a long list starting on page 65.

Meanwhile, here's an example of *just one* accomplishment per occupation. You'll be writing more. You'll be filling up pages in your notebook.

Accounting
Developed and enforced strong credit and collection policies that reduced receivables by 20% or $50,000.

Administration
Reduced stationery costs by 15%, saving $30,000 annually by initiating a competitive bid process and selecting a new supplier with lower shipping minimums.

Advertising
Improved Brand X's top-of-mind awareness 10% over the past
3 years based on annual tracking study.

Banking
Reduced bad debt from write-offs by 4% in the residential
sector by improving the screening process at local branches.

Consulting
Developed a loss prevention program which reduced warehouse shrink from 4% to 1.5%.

Customer Service
Established a staff training program that focused attention
on quicker response at the service counter with a resulting
12% increase in customers acknowledging "excellent
response time" as measured through regular mystery shops.

Direct Marketing
Implemented a new direct marketing program that increased
sales by 5% over the previous year in a flat market.

General Management
Achieved a 7% improvement in pre-tax earnings by concen-
trating sales resources against best clients and telemarketing
marginal users.

Human Resources
Reduced turnover by 12% through the introduction of
an employee satisfaction program across all stores and
central office.

Insurance
Decreased the volume of customer complaints by 53% over
three years by improving customer service staff access to
customer files.

Inventory Control
Reduced inventory by $500,000 by implementing JIT (Just in Time) delivery on a range of faster moving products.

Marketing
Increased sales 30% over a two-year period by adding natural food products to the existing product line-up, increasing sales to our existing customer base and appealing to a broader segment of new customers.

Production Control
Implemented a control system for a low volume product with a projected savings of $75,000 per annum.

Public Relations
Developed a public relations project that included two major charities adding 15% to the base business.

Purchasing
Negotiated a 5% price reduction in acquisition costs on private label product-saving the company $45,000 per annum.

Sales Management
Increased market penetration by 25% by implementing new sales incentive programs and restructuring territory coverage.

Systems
Implemented an enterprise-wide data warehousing system that enabled an increase in sales of $2.5 million while reducing inventories by $600,000 over a one-year period.

Introduce action verbs

When writing or speaking about yourself, use action verbs that portray you as a doer, thinker, leader, and problem solver, in other words, a dynamic force in the workplace. Here's a list of pivotal terms:

Accelerated	Earned	Performed	Supervised
Accomplished	Eliminated	Planned	Systematized
Achieved	Encouraged	Positioned	
Adapted	Established	Postured	Terminated
Addressed	Evaluated	Prioritized	Tested
Administered	Expanded	Processed	Traced
Advised	Exposed	Produced	Tracked
Analyzed		Programmed	Traded
Approved	Facilitated	Promoted	Trained
Assessed	Formulated	Proposed	Transferred
Augmented	Founded	Proved	Transformed
Authored		Provided	Translated
	Generated	Purchased	Trimmed
Balanced	Grew		Tripled
Began	Guided	Recommended	
Budgeted		Reduced	Uncovered
Built	Increased	Re-designed	Unraveled
	Initiated	Re-engineered	Updated
Capped	Installed	Reinforced	Upgraded
Completed	Introduced	Re-invested	Utilized
Conceived	Invented	Researched	
Condensed		Reviewed	Vacated
Conducted	Launched	Revised	Validated
Consolidated	Led		Verified
Coordinated	Liaised	Set up	Volunteered
Created		Simplified	
Customized	Maintained	Sold	Weighted
Cut	Managed	Sparked	Widened
	Marketed	Staffed	Withdrew
Delegated	Measured	Standardized	Won
Delivered	Motivated	Started	Worked
Delineated		Streamlined	Wrote
Demonstrated	Negotiated	Strengthened	
Designed		Stressed	
Developed	Operated	Stretched	
Devised	Organized	Structured	
Directed	Oriented	Succeeded	
Doubled	Originated	Summarized	

Three proven pillars of success

There's no magic formula for finding a job. It's strictly a matter of self-awareness, self-discipline, research and hard work. If you apply yourself with determination, and have a systematic approach, you'll create your own luck.

1. **Get SMART.**
2. **Maintain your FOCUS.**
3. **Market yourself with SMACK.**

Number 1: Get **SMART**

Specific
Measurable
Attainable
Realistic
Tangible

There's no point setting impossible goals or clinging to unrealistic expectations. Don't become another Don Quixote, fighting windmills and dreaming impossible dreams. Get real. Get a job and get a life. Make sure your goals are grounded in reality, not fantasy.

Specific goals have a greater chance of being achieved than general, unfocused ideas. "I want to be happy" is not a specific goal. Neither is "I want to be a manager." Here's an example of a specific goal: "I want to work as a Category Manager with a large supermarket chain in the midwestern region."

To make your goal specific, ask yourself: *What exactly do I want to do? Where am I willing to work? When can I reasonably expect to land this type of job? Which skills can I supply and what's lacking? Why do I want this job?*

Measurable goals have definable, incremental stages. If you want to work as a Category Manager in a supermarket chain, break it down into a series of steps. Set deadlines: How long will it take for information gathering? Contacting people? Interviewing?

At what point do your measurements tell you that your goal is unattainable? Continually gauge your progress and judge your effectiveness. This way you'll be able to shift gears and go on to something else if things don't materialize.

Attainable goals always involve effort. Athletes train to win races. Students study to pass exams. Likewise, there will be certain things you must do—beyond resumé writing and interviewing—to come out a winner and land a good job.

You may need to embark on a course of self-improvement, upgrade your skills, seek strong references or join professional organizations. Whatever you do, you'll always have these new skills and connections. You'll own them and can add them to your resumé.

Realistic goals are pragmatic. They match your skills with the demands of the job marketplace. Realistic goals lead to concrete offers. But if you hold on to unrealistic expectations, your search will be long and disappointing. You'll come up tired, frustrated and empty-handed.

There's no point applying for a position as a brain surgeon if you don't have a medical degree. It's also unrealistic to cling to ideas about jobs you had in the past, since they may no longer exist in the same way you remember. That's right, Bob, "The times they are a-changin'."

For a worthwhile diversion, rent a video called *Quackser Fortune Has a Cousin in the Bronx*. It's a comedy set in Dublin at the turn of the century. Gene Wilder goes through the streets scooping up horse droppings and selling them as fertilizer. He's happy. All's well until the advent of the automobile. But he has no other skills. We won't spoil the ending.

Tangible goals are real, live options. They're concrete and doable. They are actual situations where someone is willing to pay you for labor or intellectual property. A goal is not tangible if the marketplace is oversaturated with prospective candidates. Or if the sector is in decline. When this happens, you must be ready to move on to Plan B. Recast your goals, at least for the time being. Do not waste valuable time going down dead ends. If your goal turns out to be intangible, move on quickly because you're chasing a fantasy, not a job.

Number 2: Maintain Your **FOCUS**

It's easy to get sidetracked with emotions or activities that won't get you any further.

Guard against them. Be jealous of your time. Set deadlines for yourself. Be single-minded about your goals and grab hold of opportunities that exist. **Focus!**

Finding viable opportunities starts with understanding yourself, your skills, your achievements and most important, your suitability in the current marketplace. If you need an upgrade to make yourself marketable, dive in now while you have the time. If a career shift is in order, take a gamble while you have the opportunity.

> **Find viable opportunities.**
> **Obtain relevant information.**
> **Connect with the right people.**
> **Understand your progress.**
> **Strategically position yourself.**

Use every technique available for identifying obvious and hidden jobs. Remember, not all jobs are advertised. Many are posted only in company cafeterias or on corporate Web sites.

Get out there and network with people who are in the know. Work the phone and make yourself known. Do lunch. Go to farewell parties for ex-co-workers. Gather every tidbit of information and follow up.

Drill down on company Web sites and send resumés to desirable places that aren't even advertising. It costs nothing to fire off an e-mail with your resumé attached. Be visible. It's up to you to make sure you're in the right place at the right time. Use the services of a reliable recruiter who understands your field of endeavor.

Many jobs are revealed only to search companies who are paid to do the screening and pre-qualifying. They have a vested interest in finding you a suitable position.

Obtain relevant information. Read job descriptions thoroughly to see how well you fit. Remember that you have a list of preferences too, so ask questions at interviews. You may want assurances about working conditions, benefits or hours. Make sure they match your responsibilities and lifestyle.

Connect with the right people. Network to uncover opportunities. Many people will gladly give you inside information about company expansion plans. They may know about people retiring, moving or going on parental leave. Often, companies will ask their own employees to recommend candidates and offer them incentive bonuses for new hires. Instead of hiding the fact that you're out of work, broadcast it to everyone who is part of your targeted industry.

Understand and chart your progress during the search process. Know where you stand. Take stock periodically to gauge your effectiveness. Be ready to make changes, revise your goals or make a lateral move. Not all job transitions are upward and more lucrative. And not all Plan B jobs are without their merits. A varied and diverse resumé can be a plus, showing that you can function in many situations.

Strategically position yourself. Hone your message and direct it to your target audience. You have a valuable range of skills and accomplishments to bring to the table. Present these to the right people. Be visible. Be persistent. Stay top-of-mind with those in a position to hire you. Link your skills and credentials to their needs and the jobs they have open. Give them compelling reasons to choose you over other candidates.

Number 3:
Market Yourself with **SMACK**

You are about to undertake a major marketing campaign to raise people's awareness of you and your desirable character-istics. In many ways, you are like a product on a shelf. You are a brand, competing with similar brands. You need to break through the clutter to communicate your unique points of difference and com-petitive advantages.

Strong communications
Meaningful messages
Accomplishment-rich
presentation
Concentrated effort against
interested buyers
Knowledge-based tactics

Target your message to a specific audience and trumpet your features and benefits. Tip the balance in favor of being selected. Strive for impact and memorability. Here are the key components of your marketing campaign:

Strong communication pieces capture attention when they are clear, direct and impactful. They promise a valuable benefit to their intended audience. Be sure your resumé, cover letters and phone conversations are succinct, to the point and compelling.

Meaningful messages ring a bell. They resonate with the target because they say what people want to hear. So lis-ten well and thoroughly research companies of interest. Work to understand them so you can present your skills in ways that get employers' heads nodding. Practice speaking and writing from their perspective. This way you will be able to show that you understand their needs. Take a problem-solu-tion approach. They have a problem, you have the solution.

Accomplishment-rich resumés grab attention quicker than merely a list of previous jobs. A well-written resumé shines a spotlight on your achievements and presents you in the most flattering light. You will be surprised to see how strong you come across.

Concentrate your efforts by targeting the button pushers who can give you an interview. This may be the Human Resources Manager in the Financial sector, the Creative Director in the Advertising world, or the Chief Information Officer in the Information Technology arena. Contact friends who can open doors.

Knowledg-based tactics have a better chance of succeeding than unfocused trawling. Interviewers appreciate candidates who do their homework, understand their business, competitors and current challenges. Before an interview, gather as much information as possible so you can speak intelligently about the company and the services it provides.

Changing careers altogether

There may come a time when you want to change more than just your job. You may want to change your profession.

> **I am always doing that which I cannot do, in order that I may learn how to do it.**
>
> Pablo Picasso

Perhaps you're a teacher who wants to become a real estate agent. Or vice versa. You may be a marketing manager who wants to become a copywriter instead. You may be a human resources manager who wants to become a psychologist. There are a number of reasons for changing professions. Here are just a few:

- Market conditions have changed and your career is in decline or redundant.
- Your profession requires upgrading and you're not willing to invest the energy.
- Your physical or mental health necessitates a slower-paced job.
- You may have been promoted as far as possible and want a new challenge.

Before jumping into a complete and radical change, there are several questions to ask:

- Why do you want to take a totally different direction?
- Are you psychologically ready for a new definition of yourself?
- Are you ready to go through a lengthy personal assessment to determine your skills, attributes and preferences at this stage in life?
- Is the new profession compatible with the lifestyle you want?
- Is the new profession currently in demand? Or is there a glut in the marketplace?

- What are the professional credentials you'll require?
- How long will it take to complete courses, degrees and professional exams?
- How will you support yourself during this lengthy period?
- Are you prepared to start over and take an entry level salary at this stage?
- How will this decision affect your family?
- Where will you find emotional support for your decision and retraining period?

If you're convinced that you're ready to invest the time, money and energy it takes to do a complete shift, talk to a vocational counselor/psychologist, government employment center coach, or visit your local YMCA to start vocational testing and exploring your re-education options.

Strike out on your own?

You may have had an unfortunate experience working with a particular company or manager. So you think the natural next step is to become your own boss. Think again.

> **Only those who dare to fail greatly can ever achieve greatly.**
> Robert F. Kennedy

The entrepreneurial option is not suitable for everyone. We often envision an idyllic, stress-free life with loads of money and free time. In reality, entrepreneurs put in more hours and have more pressing financial obligations than employees drawing a paycheck.

Consider setting up your own business only if:

- You are entrepreneurial by nature and have always been a risk taker.
- You have the financial resources necessary to sustain you through the start-up phase and the first years of red ink.
- You have identified a viable business opportunity.
- You have the necessary skills and background.
- You have researched the market and identified your competitors.
- You have written a business plan and solicited objective advice.
- You are ready to secure loans and be directly accountable for all operations.
- You are prepared to invest the time and energy required to launch and nurture a business.

Anticipate roadblocks

Experiential roadblocks. When you apply for a job, you'll be quickly evaluated on how well your skills match the position. Your background and accomplishments stand as testaments to the fact that you can handle the assignment in question.

So be realistic. Before applying for a job, do a self-assessment. How well do your experiences correspond to what's needed? Can you do the job easily? Or are there gaps in your experience that make you less than suitable?

If you don't have the right background to be considered a viable candidate, ask yourself if there are reasonable steps you can take to change this. If the job requires academic credentials, it's sometimes possible to offer equivalent experience. But if the job requires fluency in two languages and you speak only English, move on. You're not being realistic.

> *Life has a self-correcting mechanism. Things that we once thought were terrible have a way of becoming stepping stones for new discoveries.*
>
> Raymond Soh

Overcoming experiential roadblocks. If you decide to upgrade your skills, there are a number of strategies you can employ. You can take university courses to complete a degree. You can embark on a self-study program, such as an authorized securities and investments course, or you can find a mentor who will help you build a body of work to add to your arsenal of skills.

In any case, upgrading your skills takes time and commitment. But be aware that if you go back to school while drawing unemployment insurance benefits, you might jeopardize your income. Your training will be viewed as an obstacle that interferes with your ability to find work. As an option, consider taking night courses

> *If you think education is expensive, try ignorance.*
>
> Derek Bok

while you're searching. Or take an interim job while you study to gain the skills necessary to achieve your goal.

> *Keep away from people who try to belittle your ambitions. Small people always do that. But the really great make you feel that you too can become great.*
>
> Mark Twain

Human roadblocks. Self-confidence means everything in a job interview. People can spot self-assurance a mile away. They can also sense when you're telegraphing desperation, depression or demoralization, even though you're trying to put on a brave face. It's unfortunate that our self-esteem can be at its lowest when we need it the most.

Overcoming human roadblocks. You can build your self-confidence in a number of ways. Here are some recommendations:

- Have a killer resumé that you know opens doors and gets you interviews.
- Know your achievements and be ready to announce them to the world.
- Look your best. A makeover may be in order. It will give you a lift that comes across in your attitude. Invest in your appearance. Look the part.
- Take a course in interpersonal communications. Most of us are completely unaware of the ways we affect people when we speak and gesture. Let the experts point out your habits and how you can become more effective with listening techniques, affirming the statements of others, eye contact and body language.
- Enhance your speechmaking skills. It will help in interviews, with presentations and other situations especially when you're called upon to speak before an audience. Check for a Toastmasters group in your area (http://www.toastmasters.org).
- Socialize only with people who are supportive and encouraging. They might include your closest friends, significant other or support group.

- Avoid downers. Unfortunately, they might be your relatives or past-co-workers.
- Be utterly shameless. Look straight in the mirror and say: "I can't wait till tomorrow 'cause I get better looking everyday." *(Joe Namath)*
- Don't like that one? How about, "The future's so bright I gotta wear shades." *(Timbuk 3)*

> *You can eat an elephant, if you do it one bit at a time.*
>
> Robert Riley

Complete this action plan

- I am taking control and directing this change.
- I understand how my behavior links to the values and attitudes of my generation.
- I've done an exhaustive skills inventory.
- I've listed my accomplishments, job by job.
- I'm using action verbs.
- I'm setting SMART goals.
- I'm maintaining my FOCUS.
- I'm gearing up to market myself with SMACK.
- I've given preliminary consideration to starting my own business.
- I've identified roadblocks and developed strategies for overcoming them.
- I'm boosting my self-confidence daily, and damn I'm good!

STEP 3:
Building the Perfect Beast

It's time to marshal your list of skills and accomplishments and use them to build your resumé. The purpose of the resumé is to tantalize prospective employers to the point where they want to meet you. If you already have a resumé, it's time to update it and inject some pizzazz. A resumé can be written from a number of points of view. Here we'll review the most useful.

The first person who has to believe in you is you.

You may wish to write several resumés and have them ready for different occasions. If you have two career goals, then prepare two resumés, each with a different spin. You should also have a "text-only" resumé that can be copied, pasted and e-mailed, since many positions require on-line applications that are fed into databases. Fancy formatting goes out the window on this one.

Always remember, your resumé is an advertisement for you.

Your resumé may get only a casual glance because it's buried under a stack of hundreds of others, all submitted for the same position. So it has to command attention immediately and present obvious reasons why you should be chosen for an interview.

Remember, it helps to think of yourself as a brand. You're like an item on a grocery store shelf, competing with similar items in the same group. What gives one brand a competitive advantage over another? How does Coca-Cola stand out from other soft drinks year after year?

Take a moment to think about the brands you buy on a regular basis. Crest toothpaste, Gillette shaving cream,

Clairol shampoo. What kind of car do you consistently buy? Honda, Ford, Chrysler? Which cereal always finds its way into your cupboard? Cheerios, Frosted Flakes, Shredded Wheat?

All of these brands have been built. Each has a distinct, carefully crafted and recognizable image that never changes. Most important, each has carved out a niche and made a meaningful promise. Coke promises to be the real thing. Crest promises fewer cavities. Shredded Wheat promises the whole grain and nothing added.

What are you going to promise? What is the brand image that you will create that sets you apart? How will you package yourself so you're the one who is picked by the shopper— the employer looking for the ideal candidate?

The answer lies in your list of skills and accomplishments. Take a moment to write a bold sentence that encapsulates your qualifications and gives you a distinct advantage. State your specialized skill and give an example of a noteworthy accomplishment. Here are some examples:

> *Products, like people, have personalities, and they can make or break them in the marketplace.*
>
> David Ogilvy

- I am a seasoned Marketing Manager who has launched a number of new products to national prominence.
- I am an experienced Telecommunications Engineer who has designed and implemented large-scale systems for multi-national firms.
- I am an award-winning Real Estate Agent who was top producer in my territory for five years running.
- I am an outstanding Salesperson who has increased the sales of cars, trucks and SUVs to record levels.
- I am a caring Social Worker who has introduced a special program to build work-related skills for people moving up from welfare.

State your career objective

Now, declare your goal clearly and succinctly. Add a goal statement (in italics below) to the sentence you've just written. Don't be afraid to flatter your prospective employer. Here are some examples that build on the sentences above:

- I am a seasoned Marketing Manager who has launched a number of new products to national prominence. *I aspire to join the Marketing team of a forward-looking company, to increase awareness and sales for their line of quality consumer products.*
- I am an experienced Telecommunications Engineer who has designed and implemented large-scale systems for multinational firms. *I am ready to be challenged by a Fortune 500 company with mission critical communications requirements.*
- I am an award-winning Real Estate Agent who has been a top producer in my territory for five years running. *I seek to spearhead growth, and enhance the reputation of a recognized realty company in the Greater Metropolitan Area.*
- I am an outstanding Salesperson who has increased the sales of cars, trucks and SUVs to record levels. *I seek to become a pivotal part of a top selling team that wins contracts to supply leased vehicles to corporations and organizations.*
- I am a caring Social Worker who has introduced a special program to build work-related skills for people moving up from welfare. *I am ready to apply my expertise to a counseling position in a respected school, community center or outplacement firm.*

In a matter of seconds, each summary gives a clear picture of the person, his/her skills, accomplishments and objectives. More important, it gives employers a promise of what each individual can deliver.

Create your summary based on the examples above and use it at the top of your resumé, or as the opening statement of a cover letter. It's also a good starting point when talking about yourself in interviews. Keep it in mind, as it will ensure you're prepared for the dreaded, "Tell me about yourself."

Types of resumés

Chronological resumé. Gives a list of jobs starting with the most recent. Use it to show the depth and breadth of your experience.

Functional resumé. Focuses on accomplishments and core competencies. Use it to emphasize special skills, or to reposition yourself for a different career.

Curriculum Vitae. Often confused with a resumé, a c.v. is a longer version of your life and experiences, generally used in, but not restricted to, the academic world. A c.v. elaborates on your educational experience including teaching, research, grants, awards, and affiliations.

Use a c.v. when applying for a position in an academic institution, scientific or research facility, or a consulting opportunity. As with resumés, different versions of your c.v. are appropriate depending on the position you're looking for. Your c.v. would include the traditional contact information, followed by your educational background, skills and experience. Include detailed information on relevant publications and fellowships as well.

> *Invest time in your resumé. It can produce high yields in a short period of time.*

Although longer than a resumé, your c.v. needs to be clear, well-organized and concise. On a resumé, your educational experience appears near the end whereas on a c.v., it's at the beginning.

Visit the following Web site for a sample c.v. template: www.careers.ucr.edu/students/graduates/cvsample.html. Or use your favorite search engine and enter the keywords: "curriculum vitae."

The chronological resumé

This is the most popular type of resumé and the easiest to scan by people doing the initial screening. It includes your employers, job titles, dates, responsibilities and accomplishments. It begins with your last job and goes as far back as you think necessary. Ten to fifteen years is a common cut-off, but if you have a significant story to tell, as demonstrated in the following resumé, go as far back as is relevant.

Here's an example of a chronological resumé. Note the following particulars:

- Includes descriptions of companies, their size and scope.
- Describes responsibilities. Include numbers that substantate your position wherever possible.
- Education follows job descriptions. However, if you are applying for an academic job, state your academic qualifications first.
- Memberships in professional organizations come last.
- Never state your salary expectations.
- Never use "references available on request." That's a given.
- Don't list hobbies and personal interests. Save those for the interview.

Note: the following chronological resumé conforms to the style of this text and, therefore, is longer than the three pages required when presented in standard 8½" x 11" format.

MARK J. SMITH

99 Somewhere Street • Anytown, North America • 123 456
Res: (999) 555-5555 • Bus: (999) 555-5556 • e-mail: e@mail

SUMMARY

A seasoned marketing strategist with an exceptional track record for building brand, and a keen eye for identifying differential opportunity that delivers sales and profits. Over 20 years of proven success in automotive retailing, food, drug, and hospitality. Expertise in all marketing functions, retail operations, turnarounds, and business process improvement. Seeking a senior marketing position in a growth-oriented and consumer-focused organization.

PROFESSIONAL EXPERIENCE

AUTO SERVICE CENTERS INC.   **1998 – Present**
An international automotive service retailer in Canada, the U.S. and Europe, with 800 stores and sales of $950M in the year 2002.

Corporate Vice-President Marketing
An Officer of the Company, responsible for marketing in Canada and the U.S., as well as providing strategic marketing support to European operations. Specific responsibilities: strategic market planning, category management, product development, supplier relations and procurement, industry and market research, advertising, promotion, pricing. Can/U.S. Marketing budget: $20M in 2002.

- Contributed significantly to a $12M turnaround of the Company in 1998 after major losses in Europe and North America in 1997.

- Refocused Marketing and the total organization on the consumer, through implementation of category management. Achieved annual sales increases of 12% and 14% in two consecutive years.

- Transitioned from premium priced offerings to "good, better, best" product and warranty options in key categories to better serve consumer segments with different needs.

- Reduced advertising fixed cost by 20%, freeing up more dollars for media. Expanded use of radio as a complement to television; expanded flyer frequency as a local marketing activity.

- Strengthened brand position through television and radio commercials with compelling and relevant messages that communicated value, differentiated service and guarantee.

- Improved loyalty and frequency by targeting the most profitable segments and customers needing retention, identified through data mining techniques against customer database.

PURE RITE DRUG STORES   **1987 — 1997**
A national chain of 1,200 drug stores with sales of $5.2B

Vice-President Marketing Services 1995 — 1997
Responsible for pricing, market research, advertising effectiveness tracking, marketing database, sales analysis, and plan-o-grams. Served on executive committee, which reviewed and approved key marketing, merchandising, and advertising plans and programs. Also served on implementation team, re-engineering logistics, category management and store operations.

- Coordinated key projects, including direct product profitability, warehouse size requirements, and turnover targets. Produced vendor manuals communicating systems and procedures.

- Directed the measurement and validation of product cost improvement obtainable through implementation of distribution centers versus direct supply.

- Identified pricing opportunities generating contribution in excess of $1M.

Vice-President Logistics 1988 — 1995

Responsible for the flow of goods through dedicated distribution centers, wholesalers, and direct store delivery. Served on key marketing, marketing systems and POS-user committees.

- Coordinated, managed and supervised various phases in a strategic review of business with focus on industry best practice and change required to compete effectively.

- Re-engineered controlled label soda logistics improving efficiency of distribution with annualized savings of $200K.

- Developed procedures using scan data to improve flyer item selection, flyer projection and set pricing at optimum levels based on measured price/quantity relationships.

Vice-President Marketing 1987 — 1988

Served on Board of Directors, and directed the marketing function at Northern Drugs, a $200M, 120 store franchise division of Pure Rite Drug Stores. Responsible for strategic market planning, market research, advertising ($4M budget), promotion, procurement, merchandising and pricing.

- Provided marketing direction to team responsible for a 25% increase in sales and $2.5M turnaround in profitability in just over one year.

- Improved value perception through refocus on core categories, revamped flyer with stronger value statement, and heavy-up on in-store promotion.

ABC TIRE INC.   1982 — 1987

Director of Marketing 1985 — 1987

Responsible for profitability of tire and automotive product lines. Developed marketing plan; directed pricing, promotion, advertising, training, business development and expansion.

- Directed the review and restructuring of the total business designed to improve profitability and ROI.

- Recommended franchising all stores; plan implemented.

- Maximized cost effectiveness of $8M advertising budget. Postured the brand and successfully delivered increases in traffic and sales.

Manager of Retail Operations 1983 — 1985
P&L responsibility for $110M retail division, 90 company-owned stores. Prepared marketing plan, directed merchandising and advertising for 150 company-owned stores and franchises. Responsible for $12.5M wholesale parts and equipment business, procurement and sales.

Regional Manager 1982 — 1983
Responsible for the sales and profit of 40 regional ABC Tire stores. Sales $50M

FOODCO INC.   1981 — 1982
A $200M food service company; Steak Place and Frank's Pizzeria.

Director of Marketing
Responsible for strategic market planning, advertising, promotion, market research, pricing and product development for Frank's Pizzeria.

THE LEARNING STORES   1979 — 1981
A specialty chain marketing learning materials, books, toys and games.

Retail Manager
Responsibility for P&L.

METRO NORTH FOOD STORES LTD.   1973 — 1979
Store Manager/Assistant Manager 1975 — 1979
Corporate Operational Auditor 1973 — 1975

EDUCATION
M.B.A., Marketing, University of British Columbia, Vancouver
B.B.A., University of Michigan, Ann Arbor
AFFILIATIONS
North American Marketing Association
Trans-Atlantic Advertising Club

The functional resumé

This type of resumé toots your horn. It organizes your history according to your outstanding accomplishments. You may have "worked your way up" in a company, and had success in production, marketing, operations, administration or human resources. Whatever your successes may be, they are the main points of the functional resumé.

Use this type of resumé when repositioning yourself for a new career. It concentrates on the positive effects you had on past employers.

It's also highly effective when seeking a middle management or senior position, since it highlights your core competencies and promises to deliver more of the same.

Give yourself an ego boost. Write your functional resumé.

Additionally, it's a good choice if you've held a number of seemingly unrelated jobs that suggest "job hopping," since it cherry picks your experiences and makes sense of your checkered background.

Here's an example of a functional resumé. Note:

- The brief, informative and positive summary.
- Action verbs are used to begin sentences describing accomplishments.
- Accomplishments come first; employment experience second.
- Education goes last.

Note: the following functional resumé conforms to the style of this text and, therefore, is longer than the three pages required when presented in standard 8½" x 11" format.

MARK J. SMITH

99 Somewhere Street • Anytown, North America • 123 456
Res: (999) 555-5555 • Bus: (999) 555-5556 • e-mail: e@mail

SUMMARY

A seasoned marketing strategist with an exceptional track record for building brand, and a keen eye for identifying differential opportunity that delivers sales and profits. Over 20 years of proven success in automotive retailing, food, drug, and hospitality. Expertise in all marketing functions, retail operations, turnarounds, and business process improvement. Seeking a senior marketing position in a growth-oriented and consumer-focused organization.

AREAS OF EXPERTISE

STRATEGIC PLANNING

- Contributed significantly to a $12M turnaround of automotive aftermarket retailer in 1998 after major losses in Europe and North America in 1997.

- Directed the review and restructuring of the automotive retail chain, with the mandate to improve profitability and ROI. Recommended franchising all stores; plan implemented.

- Coordinated key projects in retail drug chain, including direct product profitability, warehouse size requirements, and turnover targets. Produced vendor manuals on systems and procedures.

- Directed the measurement and validation of drug chain product cost improvement obtainable through implementation of distribution centers versus direct supply.

MARKETING

- Refocused marketing and total organization on the consumer through implementation of category management.

- Achieved annual sales increases of 12% and 14% in two consecutive years.

- Transitioned from premium priced offerings to "good, better, best" product and warranty options in key categories to better serve consumer segments with different needs.

- Improved loyalty and frequency by targeting the most profitable segments and customers needing retention, identified through data mining techniques against customer database.

- Developed procedures using scan data to improve flyer item selection, flyer projection and set pricing at optimum levels based on measured price/quantity relationships.

- Identified pricing opportunities generating contribution in excess of $1M.

- Improved drug chain value perception through refocus on core categories, revamped flyer with stronger value statement, and heavy-up on in-store promotion.

- Provided strategic marketing direction to team responsible for a 25% increase in sales and $2.5M turnaround in profitability in just over one year.

ADVERTISING
- Reduced advertising fixed cost by 20%, freeing up more dollars for media. Expanded use of radio as a complement to television; expanded flyer frequency as a local marketing activity.

- Strengthened brand position through television and radio commercials with compelling and relevant messages that communicated value, differentiated service and guarantee.

- Maximized cost effectiveness of $8M advertising budget. Postured the brand and successfully delivered increases in traffic and sales.

LOGISTICS
- Coordinated, managed and supervised various phases in a strategic review of drug chain business with focus on industry best practices and the change required to compete effectively.

- Re-engineered controlled label soda logistics, improving efficiency of distribution with annualized savings of $200K.

EMPLOYMENT HISTORY

AUTO SERVICE CENTERS INC.   1997 — Present
An international automotive service retailer in Canada, the U.S. and Europe, with 800 stores and sales of $950M (year 2002).

Corporate Vice-President Marketing
An Officer of the Company responsible for marketing in Canada and the U.S. as well as providing strategic marketing support to European operations.

PURE RITE DRUG STORES   1987 — 1997
A national chain of 1,200 drug stores with sales of $5.2B.

Vice-President Marketing Services   1995 — 1997
Responsible for performance monitoring, pricing, market research and advertising tracking. On executive committee, which reviewed and approved key marketing, merchandising, and advertising plans and programs. On implementation team, re-engineering logistics, category management and store operations.

Vice-President Logistics   1988 — 1995
Responsible for the flow of goods through dedicated distribution centers, wholesalers, and direct store delivery. Served on key marketing, marketing systems and POS-user committees.

Vice-President Marketing   1987 — 1988
Served on Board of Directors and directed the marketing function at Northern Drugs, a $200M, 120 store franchise division of Pure Rite Drug Stores. Responsible for strategic market planning, market research, advertising ($5M budget), promotion, procurement, merchandising and pricing.

ABC TIRE INC.   1982 — 1987
A national chain of 150 retail automotive service stores.

Director of Marketing 1985 — 1987
Responsible for profitability of tire and automotive product lines. Developed marketing plan; directed pricing, promotion, advertising, training, business development and expansion.

Manager of Retail Operations 1983 — 1985
P&L responsibility for $110M retail division, 90 company owned stores. Developed marketing plan, directed merchandising and advertising for 150 company owned stores and franchises.

Regional Manager 1982 — 1983
Responsible for the sales and profit of 40 regional ABC Tire stores; sales $50M.

FOODCO INC.   **1981 — 1982**
A $200M food service company; Steak Place and Frank's Pizzeria.

Director of Marketing
Responsible for strategic market planning, advertising, promotion, market research, pricing and product development for Frank's Pizzeria.

METRO NORTH FOOD STORES LTD.   **1973 — 1981**
A chain of 430 supermarkets in the northeast region with sales of $3.5B.

Store Manager/Assistant Manager 1975 — 1981
Corporate Operational Auditor 1973 — 1975

EDUCATION
M.B.A., University of British Columbia, Vancouver
B.B.A., University of Michigan, Ann Arbor

AFFILIATIONS
North American Marketing Association
Trans-Atlantic Advertising Club

Avoid common errors

If your resumé is difficult to read or uses gimmicky tricks or graphics, it will be tossed immediately. People scanning resumés spend only seconds with each one and are looking for the slightest excuse to throw yours on the rejects pile.

> **This is a two-minute read, not War and Peace.**

- Format your resumé in an easy-to-read manner using a readable font such as Times or Garamond. Avoid sans serif fonts such as Arial or Helvetica. They are for headings only and can be difficult to read. Limit the use of italics. Get professional advice from a career coach or designer.
- Never pad your resumé with lengthy, rambling, irrelevant descriptions. Keep it crisp and to the point.
- Have an audience in mind and a plan for getting their attention with your credentials. You may need different resumés for different audiences.
- Make your resumé as short as possible and as long as it needs to be. Two or three pages should suffice.
- Keep in mind that your resumé is just one of many weapons in your arsenal. Personal contacts and networking can be more effective than shooting your resumé to companies where there may be no real interest in your skills.

Cover yourself

A cover letter is a formal introduction, brief and to the point. It is not a repeat of your resumé. A lengthy cover letter is annoying. Remember, the reader is looking for any grounds to discard it. Include two or three key words that differentiate you as a candidate. Here's an example:

Stephen Snelgrove, CMA
123 Northgate Crescent
Mytown, North America
L3R 8C1

April 10, 2002

Ms. Marie Smith
Senior Consultant
PeopleFind Inc.
80F Centurian Drive, Unit 1
Markham ON L3T 6X6

Dear Ms. Smith:

Please accept this letter and resumé as my application for the position of Controller, for the furniture manufacturer in Toronto listed on the CMA web site.

I am a graduate CMA with extensive manufacturing experience in finance as well as operations. Throughout my career as Controller, Manager of Production & Inventory Control, Manager of Procurement, and Manager of Cost Accounting, I worked closely with IT, maintaining and implementing information systems.

I believe I can be a significant contributor to the success of a company this size, and would appreciate meeting with you to discuss this opportunity.

Sincerely yours,

Stephen Snelgrove
Stephen Snelgrove, CMA

Identify positive references

Chances are, your references will be contacted by phone and asked to answer some probing questions about you. So it's important to agree with your former company on the official statement regarding your departure or dismissal. You'll want to be sure that the information is balanced, giving a fair appraisal of the work you did for them.

If you do not come to an agreement with your former company about how you will be positioned, you place yourself at the mercy of the inter-office grapevine. "The word on the street," could snowball into a false or unflattering obituary.

> *Our enemies come nearer the truth in the opinions they form of us than we do in our opinion of ourselves.*
>
> La Rochefoucauld

Make sure your story jibes with theirs, especially your reason for leaving. Keep it brief, positive and plausible. Never say that you were ousted in a personality conflict. Instead, say that you achieved a number of important milestones and were ready to move on to a new challenge.

Both you and your references will be asked about your weaknesses. Be honest. Often, your greatest strength can also be your greatest weakness. Perhaps your demand for discipline stood in the way of arriving at creative solutions. Or your outspokenness irritated people and you were voted off the island. Always couch your shortcomings in terms of your ongoing professional development, and the steps you are now taking to grow.

If you suspect that your former employer holds a grudge, and is torpedoing you at the reference stage, have a chat. Negotiate. Talk about what should and should not be said. You may be surprised to find that your old nemesis has some objective insights and is equally anxious that you find another job.

Develop guidelines

You should have at least 3 to 6 people who are prepared to speak about you. They could include a more senior person in the organization who had a more favorable opinion of you than your immediate boss. Regardless of whom you choose, here are a few topics you should agree upon:

Credibility. How well does this person know you? How long did you have a working relationship? What was the reporting structure?

Accomplishments. What are the things you did well for the company? What were your noteworthy contributions?

Style. What were the most positive aspects of your management style or working habits? What kind of impact did you have on other employees? Were you conscientious, honest and fair?

> *A good name is more desirable than great riches.*
> Proverbs

Weaknesses. We all have them, so don't try to deny or gloss over them. You can ask your former boss to omit them if the subject is not raised. However, if it comes up, be sure your reference sheds a positive light, perhaps saying that you over-used your strongest points (perfectionism, need for feedback, structure or process). Your references should be able to give concrete examples of the ways you are developing profession-ally (taking courses, working with a career coach, upgrading your skills).

Reason for leaving. This is the most important point to agree upon. You made a number of valuable contributions and were ready to take on a more challenging and suitable posi-tion. And that's no lie.

Call your references and alert them. Get permission before giving their names. Ask if you could briefly review the kinds of questions that may come up and the answers that would be helpful. If you do some preliminary work with your references, they'll be well prepared and more willing to support you at this crucial stage.

> *The acknowledgment of our weakness is the first step in repairing our loss.*
>
> Thomas a Kempis

Measure progress to date

- I have written a brief summary of my skills, accomplishments and career objectives.
- I have written a chronological resumé.
- I have written a functional resumé.
- I understand the need and function of the c.v.
- I have a model for writing a professional, business cover letter.
- I have prepared a plain text version of my resumé that can be copied and pasted into the body of e-mails or used for on-line applications.
- I have had several trusted people give their opinions of my resumés.
- I have enlisted 3 to 6 people who will act as positive references.
- I have agreed on reference guidelines, especially with my former employer.

> *I find that the harder I work, the more luck I seem to have.*
>
> Thomas Jefferson

STEP 4:
Launch Your Marketing Campaign

In Steps 2 and 3, we stressed the importance of viewing yourself as a marketable product, competing with similar products in the same category. This is an important difference in our approach and the pivotal point that will tip the balance in your favor.

There are plenty of books and courses that can show you how to write a readable resumé or search for jobs. But most fail to prepare you for the competitive landscape you'll encounter next. Workers have become commoditized and are often viewed as disposable or easily replaced. Your job is to define yourself as a *value-added brand* with distinct attributes that separate you from the crowd.

> *We judge ourselves by what we feel capable of doing, while others judge us by what we have done.*
>
> Henry Wadsworth Longfellow

Carve out your niche

The world is not waiting for another shampoo, orange juice, toothpaste or ballpoint pen. Yet many new products have successfully emerged from these crowded categories. Their brand managers created a *value-added story*—a compelling reason for you to try them. They knew that consumers would be attracted to a heat-activated shampoo, a calcium-enriched orange juice, a toothpaste that whitens, or a pen with gel ink.

By the same token, no one needs just another Project Manager, Investment Advisor, Corporate Trainer, Bakery Manager or Copywriter. But they *will* be attracted to a do-or-die Project Manager, a fixed-income Investment Advisor, a stand-up comedian Corporate Trainer, a gourmet Bakery Manager or a strategically driven Copywriter.

> *Good advertising does not just circulate information. It penetrates the mind with desires and beliefs.*
>
> Leo Burnett

You don't have to become something completely different to become a value-added brand. You simply have to shift your thinking and carve out a niche, positioning yourself in a brighter and more desirable light. Use your list of accomplishments to make your promise and supply a "reason to believe." Start seeing yourself as new and improved, a cut above ordinary candidates.

Sell your features and benefits

You have skills and accomplishments that are unique. Your track record stands as a testament to your talents. You have the ability to deliver on promises that others can only wish for. You have an air of confidence that lights up a room. You are a value-added brand with a competitive advantage.

All my life, I always wanted to be some-body. Now I see that I should have been more specific.

Jane Wagner

Know yourself and your resumé inside out. Be familiar with your story, and be ready to expand on your value-added features. Have interesting anecdotes that underscore your unique selling points. Stay focused on those points that support your niche and your promise. Don't go off on tangents, telling stories that don't reinforce your main message.

Saturate your target market

Women are the target for calcium-enriched orange juice. Teenyboppers are the target for gel pens. Coffee drinkers are the target for whitening toothpaste. There's no sense wasting time and money trying to sell these products to people who are not predisposed to want them in the first place.

> *Good advertising is written always from one person to another. When it is aimed at millions, it rarely moves anyone.*
>
> Fairfax Cone

So it's important that you zero in on the people who want your product. Don't try selling yourself to everyone. This is a waste of your valuable resources. Concentrate your efforts on companies that really interest you and/or require your set of skills.

To be effective, you must be persistent and thorough. Aim for top-of-mind awareness among your targets. Use all the arrows in your quiver: resumés, letters, e-mails, phone calls, networking. Hammer home your selling points. Make sure your message is always in front of them.

Maintain a database

Keep a well-organized and up-to-date record of your contacts, with names, dates and positions you've applied for. If it's been a while since your last contact, send another resumé and letter, or make a phone call. Things have a way of changing rapidly and you'll want to increase your chances of being in the right place at the right time.

Use the library—a rich resource. Most library reference areas contain a vast array of trade magazines, journals, newspapers and reference directories that should not be overlooked in any job search. Whether your search is in the area of retail, technology or engineering, marketing, advertising, or packaged goods, a visit to your favorite library will yield useful information and job leads that

> ***Knowledge is power.***
> *Francis Bacon*

you can't afford to pass up. The directories and resources you find in your public library are free. And don't forget to contact local municipal, community, or county offices for additional sources of information on employers and employment in your area. Chambers of commerce and boards of trade can also assist.

The online revolution—use it to your advantage. In the latter part of the 1990s, the job search and recruiting process underwent an enormous and irreversible change. Internet technology brought job seeker, employer and recruiter together in a sea of information providing virtually instant access to job openings. You can access job information almost as quickly as the jobs are posted on thousands of Web sites and job banks around the world. Job seekers need to become Internet savvy if they want to conduct a successful job search, respond to opportunities in a time sensitive manner and compete effectively in the marketplace.

Company information, industry information, financial results of public corporations, jobs in government and in the private sector, names of individuals you will want to contact or target are easily researched on the Internet. It is therefore vital that you are at ease with the search engines and the research processes that will enable you to access the information you need. Fortunately, there is no shortage of information available online to assist you in this venture, and with practice your research capabilities will improve quickly.

Online job banks are an enormous resource for both job seeker and employer. Enabled by Internet technology, they connect a constantly growing number of job seekers and employers. They are remarkably good at providing thorough searches for the ideal job or candidate based on a set of keywords associated with industry, discipline, place and time.

For job seekers, job banks are public domain and free, and the steps required to post a resumé online are usually easy to follow. Job bank search engines enable you to zero in on the geography, industry and type of opportunity you are looking for. Many job banks enable you to set up an automated job search that will alert you to job opportunities that meet your pre-established criteria.

Some job banks are industry specific. For instance, for fashion and apparel click on the employment button at http://www.apparelsearch.com. For teaching go to http://www.recruitingteachers.org/aboutsite/index.html. For IS/IT go to http://www.computerwork.com.

Please note that Web addresses change from time to time, so if you have difficulty with one site or another, go on to the next.

Job-Hunt at http://www.job-hunt.org is an excellent web-based job resource containing lots of useful job search advice and tips. It is organized by industry or job specialty allowing the job seeker to quickly identify job categories and Web sites of interest.

Employers and recruiters seeking to fill open jobs scan the candidate database for appropriate individuals who meet their keyword set and criteria. Job bank search engines are powerful and often produce large lists of candidates within seconds. Job seekers should take care, therefore, to include keywords in their resumés that will give them the greatest visibility. For example, if you are searching for a job as a Project Manager, you may want your resumé to include some or all of the following keywords: "strategy," "strategic," "technology," "processes," "initiatives," "communication," "planning" and "budgets." These are some of the important words used in defining your job and keywords that employers and recruiters often search on.

Whether your job search is local, national or international, Internet job banks are an invaluable resource. *The Riley Guide* (http://www.rileyguide.com.) is an excellent Internet based resource that will link you directly to a vast base of job leads and employers. Most job banks, including *The Riley Guide*, will demonstrate how to use the Internet effectively.

Examples of Canadian job banks. Lists of current Canadian job banks can be found by keying "job banks Canada" in any search engine. Alternatively, an excellent list can be found at: http://www.ijive.com/canada/jobbanks.htm

Job bank examples include:
Careerbuilder: http://www.careerbuilder.com. (Note: click on Canada.)
HotJobs.ca: http://www.hotjobs.ca
HRDC Canada Job Bank: http://www.jobfutures.ca
Monster.ca: http://www.monster.ca
Workopolis: http://www.workopolis.com

Examples of US job banks. Lists of current US job opportunities can be found by keying in "US job banks" or "USA job banks" on any Internet search engine. An address that you will want to bookmark is: http://www.jobbanks.acdjobs.com which connects you to an excellent array of sites. Click on the various sites and decide which ones are best for you.

Drill down capability will allow you to find jobs by city and region. Bookmark the sites you want to revisit. Good examples include:

America's Job Bank: http://www.ajb.dni.us
HotJobs.com: http://www.hotjobs.com
Careerbuilder: http://www.careerbuilder.com.
JobBankUSA.com: http://www.jobbankusa.com
Monster.com: http://www.monster.com

International job banks. Use your favorite Internet
search engine to uncover international job banks. *The
Riley Guide* for international job opportunities at
http://www.rileyguide.com/internat.html is also an excellent
starting point. At www.monster.com or www.monster.ca
you will find links to *monster's* broad international coverage. Alternatively, Monster's Global gateway at
http://globalgateway.monster.com will quickly connect you
to job opportunities in any of the many countries it lists.
GoJobsite, at www.gojobsite.co.uk is another example of a
job bank listing opportunities in the United Kingdom. A
pull-down menu on the home page links to jobs in other
European countries, including France, Germany, Ireland,
Italy and Spain.

Company postings. Company Web sites provide a wealth of
information specific to their businesses and often have lists
of job opportunities. Some of these jobs may not be advertised elsewhere. To navigate to corporate Web sites go to your
favorite search engine and key in the corporate name or better yet, try keying in "jobs at company Web sites" and you
will find yourself at portals that point to corporate Web
pages. You will have a wide choice of approaches and will
need to experiment a bit to find the portal or link that suits
your purpose.

One of the more comprehensive links to corporate
resources on the net can be found by navigating to
"About.com"—a popular, multi-faceted Internet site covering
a wide range of subjects. Click on "Jobs & Careers" on the
site index, then key in "company Web sites" in the "search
for" bar and click again on "Company Research" or "Jobs
at Company Web Sites." You can also reach the very useful
"Company Research" directly by entering http://www.

jobsearchtech.about.com/cs/company/index.html in your URL. From this point you will see a listing of sites or portals linking to web sites that direct you to a vast base of corporate and industry data. *Forbes Magazine* and *Fortune Magazine* are among the better sources for US corporate data. And *The Global 500* connects to some of the world's largest corporations. Key in http://www.hoovers.com to reach Hoover's Online directly. Hoover's provides volumes of information—much of it free—on over 13,500 US and international companies.

An excellent link to Canadian corporate information is *The Globe and Mail's Report on Business Magazine*. Key in http://www.robmagazine.com and select from the Top 1000 Companies, Top 300 Private Companies, Top Tech Companies, and Top Crown Corporations replete with revenue and other financial information. Click on any of the listings and you will arrive at a general information page identifying the corporate address, key contacts, telephone numbers and Web site.

Once you are at a company Web site, find the appropriate term to click on such as "careers" or "jobs" and you will generally find a list of current job openings. Many Web sites will give you the opportunity to respond, online, to advertised positions.

Job fairs, also referred to as career fairs or expos, are organized events that bring employers and candidates together at a specific time and place. They are usually industry specific and often focused on the professional and/or higher turnover industries. A single employer may run a corporate job fair in order to recruit candidates. Colleges and universities also run fairs within specific disciplines to help place their graduates.

Employers benefit from the fairs because they have the opportunity to screen large number of candidates quickly and efficiently and book follow-up interviews where there is further interest. Candidates benefit from the opportunity to network with numerous decision-making and influential personnel all in one location. Placements often result. Furthermore, networking with other job seekers may point you toward an opportunity that might have otherwise gone unnoticed.

Job fairs are advertised in the media and are best identified and planned for by searching the Internet for upcoming "job fair" or "career fair" events. Job seekers should look over the list of employers participating and the types of positions available before deciding to attend. Once you decide its right for you, a job fair can be a worthy investment of your time.

Network, network, network

No one should depend strictly on the media, including the vast resources of the Internet, to find a job. Your network, well worked, will be instrumental in moving you along the path toward the job you want.

You absolutely must develop contacts and create a network of people who can give you information, references, leads, introductions, recommendations and more. It will enhance your search exponentially and shorten the length of time it takes to find a job.

A significant number of job seekers today find their next job through networking.

Get on the phone and get in on the gossip. Invite people for lunch or coffee. Show up at other people's farewell parties. Touch base with co-workers from the job before your last one. Go to industry award shows and functions. Maintain your ties and put in "face time." Otherwise you'll be forgotten.

Pack a portfolio

Artists, journalists and photographers are not the only ones who depend on their "bag" to get them work. Depending on past positions held, a job seeker may require a well-organized portfolio of essentials that impresses recruiters and prospective employers. Here's what you can include:

- Copies of the same resumé you sent to get the interview.
- Business cards if you have them.
- Samples of your work where it's appropriate.
- Testimonials or letters of recommendation.
- Industry awards or copies of them.
- Diplomas or professional certificates.

Presentation is key. So, keep in mind that everything should work to enhance your image and reinforce your unique attributes.

Your resumé can get your foot in the door. Your portfolio can get your name on the short list.

You may wish to leave your original portfolio after an interview, or simply leave a copy. When you come to pick it up again, you'll have a chance to ask about your status.

How about headhunters?

By all means, use them. They're in the business of finding and filling jobs and have confidential information that's beyond the scope of your regular network. There are thousands of search firms in the US, Canada and internationally. Search the Internet for useful lists. *The Riley Guide* at http://www.rileyguide.com/recruiters.html is an excellent resource with online links to free directories of recruiting firms. *Recruiters OnLine Network* at http://www.recruitersonline.com lists recruiters throughout North America and internationally.

> **Two heads are better than one.**
> *Old saying*

The Directory of Executive Recruiters from Kennedy Publications is a popular resource covering the US and Canada extensively. The Canadian Directory of Search Firms by Mediacorp Canada Inc. is a comprehensive listing covering Canada exclusively. Visit your favorite library or local bookstore and discover a variety of useful publications.

Ask your friends and colleagues to refer their favorite recruiters to you. Always search for the ones most suitable to your industry. And the good news is, job searchers should never be charged for the service headhunters provide. Their fees are fully subsidized by employers seeking to have open positions filled by recruiters who have a knack for finding candidates who meet specifications and attitudinal requirements. Here's a primer on how headhunters work.

Search firms can work exclusively on retainer or on contingency, with a mix of the two often the reality.

Retainer firms are given exclusive contracts to find people at the senior level. They get a portion of their fee up front, the remainder to be paid during and at the end of the assignment, when they locate the successful candidate. Retainer firms may be huge multinationals or small shops. Generally, retainer assignments are more difficult to fill given the complexity and confidentiality characteristic of the task.

Contingency firms are paid only if they find the successful candidate. There may be a number of contingency firms working on the same assignment at once. Alternatively, a contingency firm may be assigned a search on an exclusive basis. It is in your interest to ask the recruiter if they have the assignment exclusively. Otherwise, you may find yourself competing with candidates being presented to employers by other search firms.

Employment agencies generally handle junior positions, but may be useful in your particular industry. They can be effective in finding an interim opportunity. They often take the place of human resources departments for smaller firms and are well-positioned so they know when positions become available.

All search firms receive mountains of resumés that are routinely sorted by assistants who scan them for skills and attributes. Yours may go into a database. However, there's no guarantee that the resumé you send to a multinational search firm will wind up in their branch offices. Moreover, individual recruiters may not share information about you with their associates. At the very least, make sure your resumé goes to the branch office in the city where you want to work.

Try to get an interview with a senior recruiter in a search firm. They will have a broader base of contacts than a more junior recruiter. If a face-to-face interview is not possible, send your resumé and cover letter. You may even target several recruiters in the same firm if you feel it's to your advantage. Be prepared for a phone interview that gives the recruiter a better picture of who you are, whether they know of a suitable opening at the time or not.

If a recruiter sends you on an interview, you may not know where you're going until the last minute. Employers and their search firms often keep this information confidential.

However, you'll have a good idea of the company's business, size and general location. After the interview, the recruiter will want a debriefing to see how well you met the requirements.

Try to find search firms you click with. Avoid the ones whose recruiters appear overly anxious to get you into a job —any job—just to collect a fee. Be aware that they will be sending out other candidates for the same position. It is in your interest to work with several recruiters while searching for a position. Select those whom you feel have your best interests at heart.

Never share a recruiter's confidential information about job postings with friends. It could hurt your chances of being considered for the position and may sour your relationship with your recruiter. If you know someone who "is looking," refer them to your recruiter who will appreciate the lead.

Team up with a career coach

If you have left your job or know you will be leaving in the near future, and you have a severance package that includes outplacement, take full advantage of the career coaching, counseling and services provided. It will speed up your job search, give you empathy when you need it, and a swift kick in the pants when it's called for.

Like a trusted doctor, lawyer or financial expert, professional career coaches become an invaluable part of your support network. They have your best interests at heart. They have a body of experience that makes them eminently qualified to give you tried-and-true advice. They will provide the encouragement, guidance and critique to help move you along the path toward your next position. They'll help you define your brand image, features and benefits. They'll help you whip your resumé into shape. And they may monitor your daily timetable to see if you're spending your time effectively. Most important, they will keep you motivated with the right kind of feedback.

> *He that won't be counseled can't be helped.*
> Benjamin Franklin

If you are not lucky enough to have professional career coaching as an outplacement benefit, and you cannot negotiate it into your severance package, or, if your job search is unrelated to job loss, you will have to pursue another course of action to have access to a career coach. You may ask someone else to act as your coach and mentor. It may be a former boss or peer you trust, a customer with whom you've developed a close bond, a knowledgeable relative or close friend, someone in your support group who has recently been in active job search mode, someone who has recently gone through outplacement, or your significant other. Stay away from anyone who is judgmental, overbearing or out of touch with current conditions in your industry.

Work the phones

This is the quickest way to introduce yourself and gain an interview. However, many people haven't developed enough self-confidence to simply pick up the phone and get immediate results. They'd rather remain in the background, sending letters or e-mails. However, this "background" approach makes it difficult to break through the clutter, and the letters and e-mails may be seen as a nuisance or too impersonal to elicit a response. So use the phone.

> *Success is knowing the difference between cornering people and getting them in your corner.*
>
> Bill Copeland

Here's a strategy for using it:

- Know who you're calling and address them by name.
- Introduce yourself and state your reason for calling.
- Speak clearly and succinctly so you can develop a rapport.
- Have a scripted opening and a number of responses, especially to objections.
- Listen. Be empathetic. Spend as much time with their concerns as yours.
- Keep it brief, and try to come away with your objective (appointment, interview, presentation, etc.).
- If you feel it appropriate to leave a voice mail message, make sure it is brief and that your name and telephone number are stated clearly and slowly.

Here are some openers:

"I met your CFO at the Board of Trade last week and she suggested I give you a call. She said I'd benefit by talking with you and I'm calling to see if there's any opportunity to meet."

"I've been reading about your company in the news lately and realized I have certain skills you may be looking for. I'd very much appreciate an opportunity to show you my work."

"I'm an experienced e-commerce strategist and would welcome an opportunity to meet and talk briefly about my history and how it relates to your company."

If you encounter objections, don't be discouraged. View them as opportunities to make your case now or contact the company later. Here are some suggestions:

- Listen to the response, be patient and don't interrupt.
- Don't take objections personally or get flustered. It will undermine your credibility.
- Don't be high-handed or judgmental. You're the one who wants something.
- Probe to find out what's important to the listener.
- Offer alternatives to keep the discussion open—"May I suggest that we get together after you've completed your month's end?"

Answer ads

Newspapers, Web sites and trade publications will ask you to respond by fax, letter or e-mail. They discourage phone calls and may not even reveal the name of the company offering the job.

Your chances of getting an interview are slim because the competition is intense. To increase your chances of getting a call, be sure your cover letter information correlates *exactly* with the skills listed in the ad.

Monitor ads regularly. Take note of companies that advertise continuously. They may have a high turnover rate (red flag); or are going through a growth spurt (good sign).

Don't rely exclusively on ads, and don't expect to get much of a response. Some ads are placed to comply with fair hiring policies even though the candidate may have already been selected from within. Ads do work, but you'll probably get better results by developing your personal network and keeping your ears open.

Tap into the hidden job market

Advertising is the most expensive, labor intensive, time consuming, and least attractive way for companies to find good employees. Typically, companies prefer to use the following techniques:

1. Hire from within.
2. Mine their own company databases for resumés.
3. Get referrals from existing employees.
4. Post ads on company Web site and/or on job boards (eg. monster.com ; workopolis.com).
5. Place ads in mass media such as a newspaper.
6. Hire a recruiter to do the groundwork and find the right skill set.

We strongly recommend that you make a concentrated effort to discover the many opportunities that are out there but not immediately apparent. Here are some tips:

> *The hidden job market accounts for a significant percentage of all jobs that are filled.*

- Make yourself visible. Get out and network!
- Talk to people working in a similar field and get work-finding suggestions in your industry.
- Use company Web sites and industry directories to cold call and arrange meetings.
- Ask for leads from co-workers, friends, family and members of professional associations.
- Get hold of company newsletters that may provide leads and ads.
- Talk to headhunters who are in the know about comings and goings. They may not be able to place you now but will view you as a valuable contact for later.

- Be a detective like Columbo – dogged and persistent. You're on the trail, looking for jobs that are waiting to be uncovered.
- Become more entrepreneurial about pushing yourself forward and telling your story.

Check off this list

- I have redefined myself as a value-added brand.
- I have listed and rehearsed my competitive features and benefits.
- I have identified my target market and have launched a concentrated marketing campaign.
- I have set up a database for keeping track of my contacts.
- I am scanning job boards and using the internet as a resource.
- I will rely on networking.
- I have prepared a professional looking portfolio (where appropriate).
- I have contacted several headhunters who specialize in my area.
- I have teamed up with a career coach or mentor.
- I am working the phones daily.
- I am answering ads.
- I am uncovering the vast opportunities that exist in the hidden job market.

> *In the long run, men only hit what they aim at.*
> Henry David Thoreau

STEP 5:
Ace
The Interview

Congratulations, you're on the home stretch. You were chosen over many others to be interviewed. It's natural to feel stressed when called upon to talk about yourself, your accomplishments and especially your shortcomings. You may not be accustomed to public speaking of any kind. But if you're well prepared, and anticipate the questions and responses, you'll catapult yourself to the next level.

> **When you're prepared, you're more confident. When you have a strategy, you're more comfortable.**
>
> Fred Couples

Know what they want to know

The interviewer is trying to determine if you're the right fit for the job. First and foremost, they're interested in your skills and experiences. Equally important is your attitude, work ethic and ability to adapt to the corporate culture.

Be aware that they'll size you up in the first few seconds, so be extremely careful about your appearance, your language and the way you carry yourself. If you're a Gen Xer or Nexter, be punctual and polite. Laid back can be misinterpreted as laziness. If you're a Veteran or Boomer, be sure your clothes and hairstyle are current. An outdated look can be mistaken for outdated working skills and methods.

You'll be asked questions designed to reveal your personality, management style and alignment with their business goals. Don't be afraid to ask questions. This will carry the conversation forward and demonstrate your suitability. For instance, ask about the firm's clients, ad campaign, growth plans or special projects in order to match yourself with their current activities. Don't be a bump on a log waiting to be knocked off by a round of questions. Have confidence and have input.

> *It is better to ask some of the questions than to know all the answers.*
>
> James Thurber

Never go to an interview thinking you can wing it on your charm. Do your homework, and gather as much information as you can about the company. Remember, they'll be interviewing many people and you may have to go through several interviews, working your way up the line. Your competitors will be well-dressed, well-versed and rehearsed. They won't expect employers to recognize their inherent qualities immediately. They'll be on a campaign to sell themselves.

It may be helpful to think of yourself as a political candidate running for office. Your job is to enhance your image, make an intelligent pitch and win the vote.

Employment interviews

There is a particular job opening and you are being considered. At the same time, *you* are interviewing the company to make sure it's the fit *you* want. View the interview as a two-way exchange of information.

They'll use your resumé as a discussion starter which will guide them through a talk about your abilities. They'll also ask about your lack of skills in certain areas. Don't be put off. Simply have your responses, questions, and anecdotes ready.

Listen attentively and be wary of how you answer questions. You don't have to answer uncomfortable questions directly. Gauge your answers and steer them toward your accomplishments. Take your cues from politicians at press conferences who always paint the worst scenarios in the most positive light.

> *I spend one-third of my time thinking about myself and what I am going to say, and two-thirds about him and what he is going to say.*
> Abraham Lincoln

Be aware that different interviewers have personal styles and unspoken ideas about the purpose of an interview. Some believe it's a command performance where the onus is on you to match their requirements. They'll give few clues about how the interview is going and mull it all over later. Others see it as a test you must pass or fail. Like any other test, you'll pass if you're well prepared.

From your point of view, the interview is your chance to sell your features and benefits, making sure they link perfectly with the job description. You can expect the interview to last about an hour.

Questions they'll ask

These are the most commonly asked questions. Spend some think time with them. Get out your notebook and write down your answers. Be aware that you may be meeting with unsophisticated interviewers who ask poorly-worded or inappropriate questions. Maintain your composure and answer as best you can.

- Why are you applying for this position?
- What are your strengths?
- What are your weaknesses?
- List three of your most important accomplishments.
- What kind of work environment do you prefer?
- What motivates you to work hard?
- How are you qualified for this job?
- What supervisory or management experience have you had?
- How would you characterize your supervisory style?
- The person in this position needs to be innovative and proactive. Can you describe some things you have done to demonstrate these qualities?

> *Think of the interview as your first day on the job. Your attitude should be that of an employee who's there to talk about a new project, rather than the more obsequious attitude of a candidate who's hoping to get an offer.*
>
> Nick Corcodilos

- How would you describe your communication style?
- What other than your school and job experience qualifies you for this job?
- While this position involves some specific skills (language, computer, administration etc.), it is more of a generalist position. How do you feel that your background fits into this?
- What are the personal characteristics and qualities that you would bring to this position?

- Tell me about yourself.
- What professional groups are you a member of?
- Do you prefer to work independently or in a team?
- What appeals to you about this position and/or this company?
- What did you like most about your last position?
- What did you like least about your last position?
- What do you see yourself doing five years from now?
- Do you prefer to work in a more corporate or entrepreneurial environment?
- Starting with your last job, tell me about some of your achievements that were recognized by your superiors.
- What are some things you would like to avoid in a job? Why?
- What are the things about your last job that you feel you've done particularly well?
- What does success mean to you? How do you judge it?
- Who or what influenced you most with regard to your career objectives?

> **Don't let the interview turn into a rote question and answer session. Focus on what you can do for the employer.**
>
> www.asktheheadhunter.com

- What traits or qualities do you feel could be strengthened or improved?
- What kinds of things do you feel most confident in doing? What kinds of things do you feel somewhat less confident in doing?
- What are some of the things you are either doing now or have thought about doing that are self-development activities?
- Tell me about a time when you had a stressful situation at work and how you dealt with it.
- Customers frequently create a great deal of pressure. What is your attitude toward customer service?
- Describe a time when you were under pressure to make a decision. Did you react immediately or take time in deciding what to do?
- What types of things make you angry? How do you react?

- How do you react when you see co-workers disagreeing? Do you become involved or hold back?
- How would you deal with a difficult co-worker?
- Do you prefer to have a job in which you have well laid out tasks and responsibilities or one in which your work changes on a frequent basis?
- In your current position, what types of decisions do you make without consulting your immediate supervisor?
- Describe a situation you had with a difficult customer. How did you handle it?
- What important goals have you set in the past, and how successful have you been in working toward their accomplishment?
- What things give you the greatest satisfaction?
- What do you know about our company?
- Why do you think we should hire you?
- What will your last supervisor tell me are your two weakest areas?
- If you were hiring someone for this job, what qualities would you look for?
- What does the phrase "team leader" mean to you? When have you successfully used teamwork to accomplish a task?
- How did you organize your work in your last position? What happened to your plan when emergencies came up?
- Describe how you determined your priorities on your last job.
- Describe how you schedule your time on an unusually hectic day. Give a specific example.
- If we had to contact your staff from your previous position, what do you think they would say about you?
- How would you deal with an employee who is repeatedly late?
- How would you deal with a difficult employee?
- What was your greatest working achievement?

Innocent questions?

Seemingly friendly questions may have ulterior motives. Make sure you understand the interviewer's reason for drawing you out on certain subjects. Have replies ready that put positive spins on your history. There's a difference between *what they ask* and *what they're getting at*. For example:

Why did you leave your last job? They're on a fishing expedition. They want to know if you had trouble getting along with your boss or co-workers. They can pose the same question several ways: Were you dismissed or did you leave on your own? Did you grow tired of the job? Did you have problems fitting in with the culture? Is there anything about you or your last job that could interfere with this job?

Where do you see yourself in five years? They want to know if you'll stay or move on quickly. They want to determine if this job is an important destination for you or just a stepping stone.

> *The real art of conversation is not only to say the right thing at the right place but to leave unsaid the wrong thing at the tempting moment.*
>
> Dorothy Nevill

What kind of office equipment have you worked with? They're really asking if you're up-to-date with current technology.

Why do you want to work here? They're curious about how well you understand the company and value the position in question.

How do you feel about working long hours or weekends? They want to know if you're a clock watching nine-to-fiver or a flexible worker.

What are your strengths? They want to see how confident you are about your skills and ability to fit into the organization.

What are your weaknesses? They want to see if you're honest and aware of your shortcomings and have taken steps to remedy them.

We strongly recommend writing down your answers to all these questions plus any others that pose difficulties for you. It's not unusual for interviewers to put you in uncomfortable positions to see how you react. Be ready for the tough ones:

- Were you fired from your last job?
- How would you feel about being supervised by someone much younger than yourself?

Illegal questions

There are certain questions that should never be asked, since they can lead to discriminatory practices and violate your human rights. Common questions include: Are you married? How old are you? Do you have any children?

These personal matters may have little or no bearing on your ability to perform a job. Yet many interviewers, out of curiosity or ignorance, ask anyway. Be careful how you respond. If you object strongly to inappropriate questions, you may appear defensive or offend the interviewer. Handle the situation with tact. Instead of blurting out: "That's illegal and I don't have to answer that!" try, "How does this relate to the job?"

> *Marital status, child care arrangements, religious practices— these have nothing to do with your ability to do the job.*

You may decide to give out a bit of information without compromising yourself. If asked your age, you could state the obvious with a positive spin: "I'm in my fifties and have a track record of experience I think you'll find valuable."

If they continue to push in this vein, a stronger response can send a stronger signal: "My personal life is not a factor in this interview, is it?" or, "I was under the impression that it's illegal to ask such questions."

If you find yourself confronted by a situation you think is illegal, and you're uncomfortable, terminate the interview politely. Write a brief letter to the president of the company and send a copy to the district human rights commission.

Questions you'll ask

Be sure you walk away from an interview with a complete understanding of the duties and responsibilities of the job. Also, ask who you'll be reporting to. Later, get a fix on this person's reputation. Your network could save you from working in a place where there's potential for a poor fit.

Other questions can cover:

- Job location and company moving plans.
- Company merger or acquisition plans.
- Title, qualifications needed and professional development expected.
- Is there a job description available?
- Accountability and reporting structure.
- Organizational structure (hierarchical or flat).
- Management styles.
- Level of contact with upper management.
- Ability to have input in the decision-making process.
- Frequency of performance reviews, rewards and sanctions.
- Internal opportunities for advancement.
- Base salary, holidays, benefits, training, recognition programs.
- Performance-linked salary, commissions and bonuses.
- Financially-assisted higher education.
- Expectations about overtime and travel.
- Workplace conditions and equipment.

> *Asking the right questions takes as much skill as giving the right answers.*
> Robert Half

Information interviews

Visibility in the job search process is one of the keys to success. Information interviews serve the purpose of providing you useful information about a company or industry. At the same time, you're making yourself known, advertising your capabilities, and developing your network. Be mindful that someone is doing you a favor, so keep it short and to the point—no more than a half hour.

You can set up an information interview by calling a company that interests you. Ask to speak to a person you learned about through your network or try Human Resources. Open with something like: "Hello, my name is Joseph De Niro and I'm interested in knowing more about your company. I'm not pursuing a job at this time but would appreciate a few minutes with someone who could answer some questions about the business. Is there anyone there who might help me?"

> **You can see a lot just by listening.**
> Yogi Berra

You can also try walking in off the street and asking the same question. Many smaller companies will be glad to give you a brief tour and overview.

Information interview guidelines

When you meet with someone for an information interview, make it clear that you're not looking for a job, but only gathering information. If they think you gained entry on some pretext, and are really job hunting or trying to get an interview, they'll see you as sneaky and underhanded. Don't offer them your resumé or ask if you can send it later. Avoid leaving the impression that you're pushy.

This is a fact-finding session. So do your part and come prepared. Don't expect someone to spend their valuable time educating you. Do as much background work as possible and then concentrate on a list of prepared questions. Take notes and glean information that can turn into leads later. Your objective is to come away with general ideas about moving forward. Your questions might include:

- Could you describe the job functions in your department?
- Which areas are growing, which are in decline?
- How has technology changed the ways people perform their tasks?
- How has globalization affected change?
- Do you anticipate consolidation, takeovers, mergers?

The information interview is not a formal interview but will give you practice going into company offices, asking questions, gaining confidence and making contacts. Don't be surprised if you come away with insider information, tips about unpublished job openings and phone numbers of people to call. But remember, this is gravy, not your objective.

Phone interviews

Many companies conduct preliminary phone interviews to learn more about you and decide if you're worth talking to in person. It's important to communicate your energy and enthusiasm right from the start, since the caller will form an immediate opinion based on your voice. Answer questions succinctly, and reiterate your unique features and benefits. The longer the call lasts, the better it is for you. This indicates an interest in taking things to the next level—the personal interview.

If the job is in another city, the company may use phone interviews to keep a lid on travel costs. Always answer with respect since you may be speaking to the big cheese instead of an assistant.

> **The true spirit of conversation consists in building on another man's observation, not overturning it.**
> *Edward Bulwer-Lytton*

If you get a call that takes you off guard, ask if you can call back in 10 minutes. Give yourself time to compose yourself and go over your features and benefits. Better yet, always have your resumé close to the phone along with a few scripted responses. If they ask if you have any questions, impress upon them that you're interested in the position and would appreciate meeting face to face.

If you're not home when they call, make sure the answer on your machine sounds professional. Erase any cutesy music, kids voices or silly remarks. Simple is best – "Hello, you've reached Jean Applebee. I'm sorry I missed your call. If you leave a number, I'll get back to you as soon as possible."

Think twice about putting your cell phone number on resumés or cover letters. There's nothing more annoying for prospective employers than hearing beeping, dying batteries, a faint voice or one that drops out of range.

Screening interviews

Human resource managers may do twenty interviews a day, looking for basic qualifications that can advance candidates to the next level. They do the initial screening but are not the ultimate decision makers. They may not be well-versed with the skills needed to perform your job, so if your resumé doesn't match perfectly with the description in front of them, you could be overlooked.

> *Your objective is to get past the gatekeeper so you can talk to the button pusher.*

If you find yourself in a screening interview, don't be surprised if it seems impersonal and detached. It is. Don't be discouraged if you encounter uneducated questions and remarks. It's your job to impress the interviewer sufficiently so you can move up the line. Concentrate on demonstrating that your qualifications and experience put you in an ideal position to handle the job.

Structured interviews

The interviewer comes with a list of questions prepared in advance. Each candidate is asked the same questions in the same way. The interviewer has a mental picture of the perfect employee, but this is not revealed to the candidates.

If you find yourself in a structured interview, you'll be graded on how well you fit the ideal attributes and attitudes. You'll never know what they're aiming for or how well your foot fits into Cinderella's glass slipper.

> **Do: Arrive early. Dress smart. Listen. Be prepared. Focus on what you will do for the company.**

Don't be afraid to answer honestly and boldly. If you say you're a stickler for strategy or process, you may hear a sigh of relief because that's exactly what they're looking for and the reason the previous person is out of a job. This is not the time to be overly polite, reticent or non-communicative. Sell your features and benefits aggressively, hoping that you fit the bill. If you don't fit, don't worry. The job wouldn't have suited you anyway.

Phases of the structured interview

The introductory phase may seem casual but it is crucial. Even though you're making small talk about the weather, you're being judged on your appearance and demeanor. More than 80% of all communication is non-verbal. An interviewer will form an opinion in seconds, according to your manner, not your knowledge.

Ask yourself what messages you're communicating with your clothing, handshake, posture and body language. Always wait for an invitation to sit down. Don't hold your briefcase on your lap, rest it on the floor. Be friendly and open. Don't slouch; this signals disinterest. Don't fold your arms in front of your chest; this projects a closed and defensive attitude. Engage the interviewer by leaning forward, listening and responding in ways that show you're following their train of thought. Save your questions for appropriate moments.

> *Don't: Leave your cell phone on. Answer questions without pausing to think. Try to negotiate a salary.*

The middle phase will be filled with questions about your skills and background. Keep your answers articulate and to the point. Don't ramble. Again, it's not what you say, it's how you say it. Don't hijack the conversation so you can launch into your pitch. Wait for the appropriate openings.

The closing phase leaves room for you to ask any unaddressed questions. Touch on any of your strengths that may not have been discussed. You may ask when the final decision will be made and if it's appropriate to call. Thank the interviewer by name, offer a firm handshake and leave cleanly. Don't drag things on with additional dialogue.

Unstructured interviews

Smaller companies may not have lengthy job descriptions or a profile of the ideal candidate. They're simply looking around to see who's out there before making a decision. If you're used to large, buttoned-down corporations, this type of loosey-goosey interview may seem off-putting and unprofessional. They'll seem unfocused and unprepared for the interview.

You may have to explain your features and benefits in-depth without ever knowing if they're relevant. But you have nothing to lose by selling yourself hard. Even if your basic skills seem unusual to them, they may be attracted to your "soft," interpersonal skills: focus, drive and organizational know-how. You could easily become a big fish in a small pond, transferring your techniques to new areas.

Multiple interviews

If you're being considered for a senior corporate position, or an assignment in a team-oriented industry such as e-commerce, you can expect to go through a sequence of interviews. Everyone who'll have contact with you on the job will have a say in whether you're hired. Sometimes this technique is used to weed out people at various stages, similar to a game of "Survivor."

Q: Why can't I just be myself in interviews? A: Because this is a special situation where you show only certain aspects of yourself in order to get what you want.

The trick is to form a relationship with each interviewer, and tailor your pitch to their point of view. Competency and credentials may be important to one person, while flexibility and well-roundedness may be important to someone else. Use your listening skills to pick up on their areas of interest and spin your story to assure each person that you make the best fit.

Stress test interviews

Fasten your seatbelt. Stress interviews are meant to be unnerving and confrontational. They're designed to put you in the hot seat where your reactions can be watched. There may be two people firing questions and not waiting for you to finish your replies. There may be long, uncomfortable pauses. This is a set up, calculated to upset you and watch you perform under pressure.

> *No matter how unsettling, never become defensive, argumentative or rude.*

As soon as you recognize the stress interview, you can relax because you understand the game. You don't have to rise to the bait, squirm, become angry or defensive. You don't have to let them wear and tear you down. Simply maintain your composure and be ready for a battery of predictable but outrageous questions:

What are your weaknesses? Turn this one around with answers similar to: I'm a perfectionist. I'm too punctual. I demand results. I insist on quality. I always seek consensus. I call it like it is.

There's a gap in your resumé. Why haven't you worked in the past year? Make yourself desirable, discriminating or busy with important activities: "I've turned down several offers because I'm pursuing a career, not a job." Or, "This was a scheduled sabbatical, dedicated to travel and professional development." Or, "I was successful in the stock market and took profits to allow myself time to find the right company."

Why should we hire you? Briefly state your qualifications, weaving them into their job description. If you don't have much experience, show that your educational background prepared you well for the job. Never say that you need the money. Cast everything in terms of their needs.

What to do if:

Two interviewers start shooting rapid fire questions. It may be useful to see yourself as a political candidate being heckled. Take control by slowing down the process. Try: "Thank you. I'll get to your question when I've finished answering Mr. George." Or, "Which question would you like me to answer first?"

There's a long, pregnant pause. Wait calmly. This technique is used to see how you react to uncomfortable situations. Resist the temptation to speak. You could be putting your foot in your mouth. Remember, this is their game, so let them break the deadly silences. They will rarely pause for more than 15 seconds.

> *Stress interviews are routine for people who will be in the public eye or working in a pressure cooker.*

They become confrontational. "We're not convinced you meet the requirements of the job." Sit tight. This is their ultimate attempt to rile you. You wouldn't be in the interview if you didn't have the right qualifications. They want to know if you have a short fuse. Relax and respond with: "Really? Could you elaborate on that?" Send the ball back into their court.

Behavioral interviews*

"Tell me about a time when you were on a team, and one of the members wasn't carrying his or her weight." If this is one of the leading questions in your job interview, you could be in for a behavioral interview. Based on the premise that the best way to predict future behavior is to determine past behavior, this style of interviewing is gaining wide acceptance among recruiters.

Today, more than ever, every hiring decision is critical. That's why behavioral interviewing is designed to minimize personal impressions that can affect the hiring decision. By focusing on the applicant's actions and behaviors, rather than on subjective impressions that can sometimes be misleading, interviewers can make more accurate hiring decisions.

James F. Reder, Manager of Staff Planning and College Relations for Occidental Chemical Corporation in Dallas, says, "Although we have not conducted any formal studies to determine whether retention or success on the job here has been affected, I feel our move to behavioral interviewing has been successful. It helps concentrate recruiters' questions on areas important to our candidates' success within Occidental. The company introduced behavioral interviewing in 1986 at several sites and has since implemented it company wide."

* This section on Behavioral interviews has been reprinted with the kind permission of the University of North Carolina at Chapel Hill, University Career Services.

Behavioral vs. traditional interviews

If you have training or experience with traditional interviewing techniques, you may find the behavioral interview quite different in several ways:

- Instead of asking how you would behave in a particular situation, the interviewer will ask you to describe how you did behave.
- Expect the interviewer to question and probe (think of "peeling the layers from an onion").
- The interviewer will ask you to provide details, and will not allow you to theorize or generalize about several events.
- The interview will be a more structured process that will concentrate on areas that are important to the interviewer, rather than allowing you to concentrate on areas that you may feel are important.
- You may not get a chance to deliver any prepared stories.
- Most interviewers will be taking copious notes throughout the interview.

A behavioral interviewer is trained to collect data and match it to a profile. Nothing more.

The behavioral interviewer has been trained to objectively collect and evaluate information, and works from a profile of desired behaviors that are needed for success on that job. Because the behaviors a candidate has demonstrated in previous similar positions are likely to be repeated, you will be asked to share situations in which you may or may not have behaved in certain ways. Your answers will be tested for accuracy and consistency.

If you are an entry-level candidate with no related experience, the interviewer will look for behaviors in situations similar to those of the target position:

- "Describe a major problem you have faced and how you dealt with it."
- "Give an example of when you had to work with your hands to accomplish a task or project."
- "What class did you like most? What did you like about it?"

Follow-up questions will test for consistency and determine if you exhibited the desired behavior in that situation:

- "Can you give me an example?"
- "What did you do?"
- "What did you say?"
- "What were you thinking?"
- "How did you feel?"
- "What was your role?"
- "What was the result?"

You will notice an absence of such questions as, "Tell me about your strengths and weaknesses."

How to prepare for a behavioral interview

Recall recent situations that show favorable behaviors or actions, especially involving course work, work experience, leadership, teamwork, initiative, planning, and customer service.

- Prepare short descriptions of each situation; be ready to give details if asked.
- Be sure each story has a beginning, a middle, and an end. In other words, be ready to describe the situation, your action, and the outcome or result.
- Be sure the outcome or result reflects positively on you (even if the result itself was not favorable).
- Be honest. Don't embellish or omit any part of the story. The interviewer will find out if your story is built on a weak foundation.
- Be specific. Don't generalize; give a detailed accounting of one event.

A possible response for the question, "Tell me about a time when you were on a team and a member wasn't pulling his or her weight" might go as follows:

"I had been assigned to a team to build a canoe out of concrete. One of our team members wasn't showing up for our lab sessions or doing his assignments. I finally met with him in private, explained the frustration of the rest of the team, and asked if there was anything I could do to help. He told me he was preoccupied with another class that he wasn't passing, so I found someone to help him with the other course. He not only was able to spend more time on our project, but he was also grateful to

The questions are predictable. But your answers require intense preparation.

me for helping him out. We finished our project on time, and got an 'A' on it."

The interviewer might then probe: "How did you feel when you confronted this person?" "Exactly what was the nature of the project?" "What was his responsibility as a team member?" "What was your role?" "At what point did you take it upon yourself to confront him?" You can see it is important that you not make up or "shade" information, and why you should have a clear memory of the entire incident.

The thank you letter

This simple courtesy can have tremendous effects and tip the balance in your favor. Yet most people rarely use it. A formal "thank you" shows you respect the interviewers and value their time. It also demonstrates that you possess the kind of people skills your competitors lack.

> *You can break a tie between yourself and another candidate with a formal thank-you note. Snailmail is better than e–mail.*

Structure the letter with a brief thank you, a highlight of one of your most pertinent skills, and an invitation to call you back. Send it on good stationery within 24 hours of the interview. See sample on the following page.

Betsy Harrare
123 Somewhere Street,
Anytown, North America 12345

July 24, 2002

Mr. Ivan Stanton
Cando Industries
57 Which Street
Yourtown, Anywhere L3S 4W1

Dear Mr. Stanton:

Thank you for taking the time to meet with me today. I was pleased to share my vision of how my skills might become valuable assets to Cando Industries.

I appreciated the opportunity to tour the plant and was struck by the cultural diversity at your company. You mentioned that there was no one on your management team who spoke anything but English. As I mentioned, I'm fluent in Spanish and French, as well as English, and would welcome a chance to improve your internal communications.

This, and other capabilities, make me confident that I can make a significant contribution to Cando. I look forward to speaking with you again and am available for any further questions.

Sincerely yours,

Betsy Harrare

Betsy Harrare

Call backs

If you're invited back for a second or third interview, consider yourself close to an offer. They may have questions they want to clarify or simply want a last look before they make a decision. They may also be comparing you to other candidates who have been called back. Don't relax.

Do more research on the company and come back with your own questions. Find fresh ways to sell your features and benefits based on what you learned in the last interview. If you're being interviewed by a different person than before, develop a rapport by listening carefully to that person's needs. Position yourself as the brand of choice for the job.

> **What has become clear to you since we last met?**
>
> Ralph Waldo Emerson

Storytelling

Would you like an edge over other candidates with similar skills and experiences? Would you like to add an ingredient to your interviews that makes you the most memorable? Then tell a story.

Everyone loves a good story and many successful TV commercials use stories to sell products. Stories peak curiosity, hold interest and reinforce the brand image. Your story will be recalled later to cull the herd of candidates and provide a benchmark for your future performance.

Superman, Wonder Woman, James Bond or Zena. Have at least two or three good stories where you were the hero who saved the day.

Your story can be informative, humorous, inspirational, ironic or bizarre. The important thing is that it demonstrates your special features and benefits. If there's a natural place in the interview to tell your story, take advantage of it.

HOW TO SPIN A GOOD STORY

Set the scene with a vivid description of the problem.
"Market share was plummeting. We were down considerably in the second quarter. Our widgets were heading south and no one knew why."

Develop the plot with yourself as the leading character.
"I knew we were in serious trouble and realized we weren't communicating our benefits over other brands. I knew we had lower warehousing costs and could undersell the competition. But there was no time to simply reduce prices and hope for the best. I proposed that we hire a local radio personality to promote our benefits and prices on his morning show."

Get to the climax.
"Our sales shot up 14% in the next quarter. The only thing we did differently was run my ad campaign. I was recognized at the regional sales meeting, where they surprised me by having the radio announcer present me with an award."

Summarize, interpret, make promises about the future.
"I really enjoy solving problems and looking for creative solutions. I identified closely with my last company and took their challenges to heart. Lots of people leave problems at work, but I get a kick out of coming up with ideas to turn things around. I'd like to continue having this kind of positive effect."

> *Never tell the moral of the story. Let them make up their own minds.*

Never sum up with something tactless.
"I'm convinced that the true story I just related proves that I'm dedicated and perfectly suited to the position, and that I'm the person you should hire." Never be pompous and self-serving. You can influence their thinking, but don't try and make their decisions for them.

Your clothing is your packaging

A top quality product never succeeds in the marketplace without the appropriate packaging, and neither will you. Your clothing speaks volumes about you before you even open your mouth. Always dress for the position to which you aspire. If you look the part, you'll give people confidence in your ability to do the job.

Dress appropriately for your industry. Always opt for a more conservative image. Clean, well-pressed clothes make a difference and so do shined shoes. Dirty hair and nails are an immediate turn off. Freshen your breath but don't chew gum. Leave yourself enough time to arrive early, use the washroom and check yourself in a mirror. Be polite to receptionists because they often have influence.

Business women do well with dark suits and blouses. Avoid cleavage, miniskirts, flashy jewelry and loads of accessories. Stay away from perfume and heavily scented deodorants, as many people suffer from allergic reactions. Bare legs are a no-no, dress shoes are a must. Keep make-up and nail polish natural looking, or it will be distracting. Get a good simple haircut that suits you. Don't juggle a briefcase, handbag, portfolio, umbrella, etc. Try to have one, well-made leather bag that carries everything. If you need an overall picture, rent the video *Working Girl*. Melanie Griffith is the *don't*. Sigourney Weaver is the *do*. One last thing: check for trailing toilet paper when you leave the restroom (this one is for the men, too).

> **Nothing succeeds like the appearance of success.**
> Christopher Lasch

Business men will do well with dark, wrinkle resistant suits. Navy or gray works well but browns and tans don't. Shirts should be crisp and long-sleeved. Avoid polyester. Choose ties and socks that complement rather than match. Wear dark leather shoes. Check for gum on the soles.

Business casual. Try to find out the dress code of the company where you're being interviewed. Many have loosened the rules and have gone "business casual." This doesn't mean anything goes. Business casual is a difficult look to achieve, since it's less formal than traditional business attire but dressier than your weekend clothes. Good quality knit sweaters have replaced shirts and ties for men. Sports jackets with sports shirts are recommended. Women can opt for tailored slacks but not jeans. Bare midriffs, sandals, sweats and tube-tops are inappropriate and will damage your credibility. In fact, many Fortune 500 companies are going back to formal business attire, so don't make yourself uncomfortable by showing up looking too casual.

> *Dress like a bum and you act like a bum. Dress like a gentleman and you act like a gentleman. Clothes create an impression you must live up to.*
> Jack Wood.

Of course, industries such as advertising, new media and film have their own dress codes. Traditional business attire shows that you don't fit in. Look for sleeker designs that flatter you. You'll never go wrong with basic black because it's the standard uniform. But don't show up covered in lint, dandruff and dog hair. Pay special attention to your accessories. They define your brand image and send a message about the caliber of creative work you provide. Keep jewelry and watches simple and sophisticated. Save the nose rings for the club scene.

Don't leave home without...

- Knowing the job description in-depth.
- Having a list of your own questions.
- Having an extensive list of answers to typical questions.
- Knowing the difference between what they ask and what they're getting at.
- Understanding human rights legislation.
- Knowing the different types of interviews and being prepared for each: *Employment, Information, Phone, Screening, Structured, Unstructured, Multiple, Stress, Behavioral.*
- Having a ready supply of responses and details for the behaviorists.
- Having appropriate stationery for thank-you notes.
- Having two or three good stories that cement you in their minds.
- Being scrupulous about your appearance and manners.
- Checking the dress code of the company where you're being interviewed.

> *You must have a high concept not of what you are doing, but of what you may do someday. Without that, there's no point to working.*
>
> Edgar Degas

STEP 6:
Negotiate
The Offer

You nailed it! They made you an offer. It's euphoria, relief and cloud nine all rolled into one. But once again, we ask you to separate your emotions from the task at hand. Before accepting willy-nilly, there's one last step to complete. You must evaluate and negotiate the offer.

> *Take care to get what you like, or you will be forced to like what you get.*
> George Bernard Shaw

You may not be experienced with negotiating, and most are notoriously ill-prepared to play this game. Negotiating seems like a secret skill known only to the Donald Trumps of this world. But it's no mystery. There are certain points you should be familiar with to ensure the offer fits your requirements now that you've fulfilled theirs.

Does the offer reflect market conditions?

Offers are not made in a vacuum. They're a function of supply and demand. A number of factors are taken into consideration when a company makes an offer of employment: general economic conditions, market trends, available talent pools and revenue forecasts. You should be up to speed on everything so you can assess their position, and gauge your leverage.

Know the overall industry. It's critical that you have an overview of the general sector and its stage in the business cycle. Is it on an uptrend or down-swing? Is it a growth industry or a mature industry? If you accept an offer in a volatile industry such as new media, you could easily get caught in a round of layoffs if there's a sudden shift in market sentiment. Weigh the risks and rewards. Have a back-up plan. If the company is part of a mature industry such as pulp and paper, you'll probably have more stability. On the other hand, entrenched business practices and a rigid corporate style may prove insufferable if you have an entrepreneurial spirit.

> *In the end, more than they wanted freedom, they wanted security.*
>
> Edward Gibbon

Know the company. What's their position relative to the competition? Are they a respected leader in the industry? Or a B List player? What's their financial position? If they're a publicly traded company, get a copy of their annual report. It's free, and available online or by mail. Skip the marketing bumf up front and scrutinize their balance sheet. What are their costs of doing business? What's their debt load? And most important, what's their share price? The stock market decides a company's worth, and a simple historical chart will give you an instant picture of their peaks and valleys over time. Check out their stocks online.

Next, gather as much information as possible about the corporate culture. Tap into your network and catch the buzz. Talk to current and ex-employees, if possible. Try to get a fix on the prevailing morale. Are there people to watch out for? Why did people leave? If the environment is rigid and closed, it may not bode well for someone with talent, enthusiasm and ideas. Conversely, if the environment is flat and entrepreneurial, it may not be the best fit for someone who needs structure and a defined hierarchy.

> *No sensible decision can be made any longer without taking into account not only the world as it is, but the world as it will be.*
>
> Isaac Asimov

Know the competition. Is the company in a strong position to maintain or increase their market share? Or are they getting hammered? If they're vulnerable, they may become the target of a takeover bid, in which case you could be redundant and out the door *tout de suite*. However, if the company is in rough shape, and you want to help turn things around, make sure the offer reflects the risk you're taking. Stock options, performance bonuses, signing bonuses—these are the most common sweeteners.

Elements of the offer

Don't be content with a short letter that offers you a title, salary and paid holidays. There are a number of components that should be included in a well-defined offer.

Salary. How will you be compensated? There may be an annual salary or a base salary plus commissions. Be sure your monthly compensation meets your financial needs. Factor in federal, state or provincial taxes, benefits you pay for, and any other deductions. Compare your take home pay with your monthly expenses in Step 1.

> **"I know but I had a better year than Hoover."**
>
> *Babe Ruth's reply when a reporter pointed out he was asking for more money than the President.*

Be sure the salary they're offering is fair. Compare their offer with going industry rates. Also, get objective opinions from your network. Don't be shy about talking money. It's not a four letter word or a deep dark personal secret. Check for salary ranges on relevant Web sites.

Bonuses. They come in all shapes and sizes and vary considerably among similar companies in the same industry. Be sure you know the rules and how you'll be evaluated. Some criteria are impossible to achieve. Ask how your bonus might be split between company performance and personal performance. Ask about past payouts for positions similar to yours.

Be careful of starry-eyed stories about stock options. There's no guarantee they'll be worth anything when you want to cash out. Ask if the company has a loan policy so you can buy them. That's right, you have to buy the stocks before you can sell them at a higher price. It could cost thousands, and your profits will be subject to tax. A stock option is nothing more than a *chance* to buy their stock at a specified price. And you'll need a lot of ready cash to do it.

Signing bonuses are another flavor, and a one-time incentive to join the company. Don't be flattered or sucked in. If you have two offers, compare them without the signing bonus. It should have little bearing on your decision.

Less exotic bonuses may be more tangible and rewarding. There may be an annual incentive bonus based on your salary or sales. There may be a profit-sharing plan or a retirement program where the company matches your contributions. Interview current employees, if possible, about potential problems. A retirement plan might be "locked in" and untouchable until you reach a certain age. Or, an "investment program" may not offer many investment choices beyond the poor performers of a single mutual fund company.

> *I'm gonna make him an offer he can't refuse.*
> Don Corleone

Bonuses should never be deal breakers. They're extras. But this doesn't mean they should be taken for granted or glossed over. Investigate thoroughly. The more you know up front, the fewer problems you'll have. You can't complain later about getting a raw deal if you didn't bother to find out what you were signing up for.

Benefits. Most companies have a plan of some kind. Hospital, dental and drug costs are covered by basic plans. Find out *how much* is covered. They may pay only 50 – 80% of the costs, and only after a long waiting period before you become a plan member. See if there's life insurance and how much.

Ask if they have a more comprehensive or flexible plan that goes beyond the basics. You may want out-of-the-country medical coverage, eye care or orthodontic coverage. You may want more personal life insurance or policies on your family.

Be prepared to have deductions taken from your salary since the company may pay only a portion. Keep in mind that if you leave the company, you leave the coverage behind. It may be cheaper for you to buy life insurance on your own than to watch your premiums go up as you leave jobs and grow older.

Non-financial benefits. These may include fitness memberships, trips to conferences, support for higher education,
subsidized cafeteria meals, mem-
berships in associations and so on.
These perks are not substitutes for
salary and will not improve your
cash flow. View them as nice-to-
haves but non-essentials.

> *Every day I get up and
> look through the* Forbes
> *list of the richest people
> in America. If I'm not
> there, I go to work.*
>
> Robert Orben

Vacation. This is a bargaining chip
that could be turned into a win-win situation. Suppose you
want more money but they're not in a position to offer it
since they're working within strict salary ranges. It's worth a
try to ask for extra paid holidays instead. You'll get a better
deal and they'll have stayed within their policy guidelines.

Car or allowance. You may be given a company car, with costs
paid on insurance, maintenance and gas. Or you may be
given a monthly car allowance. Be sure you understand how
your taxes will be effected in return. At the very least, you
should be given a tax-free mileage allowance, designed to off-
set the costs of operating your vehicle.

Employment contracts

You may be offered a full-time position with a company and still be required to enter into an employment contract. In some industries, this is quite common. The purpose is to set out the terms of the working relationship and the procedures for termination, similar to a pre-nuptial agreement. The employment contract generally includes:

- Title, description of duties, reporting structure.
- Length of contract, if applicable.
- Compensation (how much and when).
- Benefits, bonuses, pension, insurance, cost of living adjustments.
- Probationary period.
- Paid vacation.
- Lead time required for either party to terminate the contract.
- A confidentiality agreement (separate document).
- A non-competitive agreement (may last for years after the contract is finished).

> *By working faithfully eight hours a day, you may eventually get to be boss and work twelve.*
>
> Robert Frost

While the contract is meant to protect both you and the employer, it can also limit your flexibility in the future. A strict job definition can quickly become dated, and you may find yourself with expanded responsibilities but without the raise in pay.

Be careful of clauses designed to prevent you from working for the competition if you leave, or restrict you if you want to open your own business. You may not have a choice, but be sure you understand the terms and conditions.

Make sure you understand the implications of leaking confidential information or stealing intellectual property.

Grounds for dismissal should be clear and linked to "cause." Otherwise, you could find yourself being marched to the elevator wondering what you did wrong.

If you are in a senior position, or your situation is complicated, you may want to talk to an employment lawyer before signing any contract.

Severance packages

At the senior level, it's common to negotiate the terms of severance for reasons other than "cause." A company may decide to terminate you because of a poor fit, issues with your management style, or other frictions that may occur. There should be a precise statement of the conditions under which you can be let go, and the compensation you'll receive. Before accepting a senior position, exercise your prerogative. Ask for a separation clause and review it with an employment lawyer before signing.

What the pro's know

So, now that you know the company and its offer in detail, it's time to deal.

You may never have negotiated anything in your life. You may hate buying a car because you never know if the price is fair. You may stay away from shopping in certain countries because you're not comfortable haggling. Okay, it's time for you to develop a new skill and get a better deal for yourself.

There's an art to making a deal and some people savor every moment, twist and turn. It's a game with its own rules and strategies. There are winners and losers. Some people make a living doing nothing else but putting together deals. There are books if you're interested, and you should be, but here are the basics in a nutshell:

Evaluate the offer

Throughout this entire process, we've asked you to put your emotions aside while you were looking for a job. Now we want you to bring your feelings to the fore and use them. Ask yourself: How does this offer make me *feel?* Excited? Disappointed? Wary? Indifferent? Undervalued?

Trust your instincts. This is the most important clue about the offer and whether you will be ultimately happy doing the job. You should feel good about accepting. You should feel comfortable with the terms and conditions. Don't be afraid to ask for modifications. And never be afraid to turn down an offer if your gut instincts tell you that accepting would be a mistake.

> *Follow your instincts. That's where true wisdom manifests itself.*
> Oprah Winfrey

Dollars and sense. Is it fair and equitable given your qualifications and the current state of the industry? Does the salary meet your basic monthly needs?

Non-financial benefits. Does the benefits package fit with your needs and those of your family? Are the perks something you value?

Terms of separation. Are you comfortable with the terms of the severance package? Does the package give you enough freedom to accept a job from the competition in the future, or strike out on your own once your relationship has ended?

Be reasonable and flexible

This is a give and take process. Negotiation is about compromise and not digging in your heels. You may not get everything you want. But you must know how far you're willing to compromise.

Your objective is to deploy your talents and become employed. To get there, you may have to accept a few clauses you don't like. Try to understand why an employer insists on certain terms. Be flexible. Things can change once you're working, when you'll be given opportunities for advancement.

> **The point is that you can't be too greedy.**
> *Donald Trump*

Pick your battles. You can negotiate any terms that have wiggle room. But you must play by the rules and do it in a fair and reasonable manner. Know your basic requirements. If you can't get them, shake hands, thank them politely and walk away. You wouldn't have been happy working there anyway.

When should you accept an offer? When you're comfortable with the overall terms, when the pros outweigh the cons.

Negotiating strategy

Negotiating an offer may be a difficult process for some people, especially those who equate negotiation with bargaining. In some cultures, bargaining is considered non-genteel; in others, it's a way of life.

It is important to appreciate that negotiating an offer is far removed from bargaining, especially when you're attempting to substantiate your value proposition. After all the work you've put into posturing your features and benefits, defining your competitive advantage, and convincing the employer to present you an offer, you should not retreat from your strengths and value. Negotiation is a matter of finding common ground, a win-win situation for both you and the employer. Keep this perspective in mind when reviewing and/or negotiating a job offer and you will likely obtain a satisfactory outcome.

> *There is no future in any job. The future lies in the man who holds the job.*
> George Crane

The most critical condition in preparing for a job offer is organization. Have a list of your requirements and a clear idea of your baseline salary position. Know your total package requirements. Understand that there may be trade-offs. For instance, you may take a lower salary in exchange for more holidays. Take the list of requirements to the meeting and check off the items where you come to an acceptable agreement.

Always have arguments and information to back up your case. If you can document the reasons why you're asking for certain concessions, you'll have a better chance of coming away with what you want.

You don't have to accept or reject an offer on the spot. Say you'll take three days to consider the revised offer and will get back to them with your decision. If it's complex, or you're considering more than one offer, go away and make a list of all the pros and cons. Be objective and get advice from those who have been supporting you through this transition. If you adopt a realistic perspective, you'll come to the best decision.

If you decide on the spot to accept the offer, shake hands and congratulate them. Let them know that you're delighted with the agreement and are looking forward to starting. They'll send you a formal offer, which you'll sign immediately and be off to the races. Well done!

Before you sign on the dotted line

- Trust your instincts.
- Evaluate the offer in terms of market conditions.
- Research the company's competitors and financial position.
- Gather information about company morale and any "red flags."
- For senior positions, be sure the offer includes a settlement package in case you're asked to leave.
- An offer of employment or contract should include specific details about:
  Title, duties, responsibilities, reporting structure
  Salary and vacation
  Performance reviews, bonuses and criteria
  Benefits and non-financial perks
  Probationary period and wait time for benefits
  Causes regarding dismissal and a pre-arranged severance package
  Confidentiality and non-competitive agreements.
- Negotiate the offer, being reasonable and flexible.
- Know your requirements, your baseline salary position and your total package requirements.
- Be ready to accept an overall deal that's comfortable.
- Have a bottle of champagne on ice for when you get home.

> *It's a funny thing about life: if you refuse to accept anything but the best, you very often get it.*
>
> Somerset Maugham

Conclusion
and Beyond

Thank you for allowing us to be part of your transition. Whether your goal was to replace a lost job or move to a new career, you now have a thorough understanding of the nuances of the job search process and the knowledge to prepare and utilize a stand-out resumé.

Your tool kit now includes an arsenal that highlights your accomplishments and positions you effectively in the marketplace. With resumés in hand (you should always have more than one), a sound understanding of the interview process, and confidence in your ability to negotiate an offer, you are now "ready for business" — you now have the materials and knowledge you need to work through the job search process effectively.

> *Success is never final.*
> *Failure is never fatal.*
> *It's courage that*
> *counts.*
>
> Winston Churchill

You also have the insight that will help you better manage your "marketing campaign." You understand the need to break through the barriers with relevant and clear communication. You understand the need to obtain face-time with prospective employers — you have a message to deliver, a message that effectively tells each and every employer that you are the right candidate for the job. Landing the right job depends on how effectively you deliver this message and how relevant it is.

No one suggested that the job search process would be an easy one. No one said it is always fair. We know the path to a new opportunity can be riddled with land mines. Roadblocks can abound—age, race, gender, weight, appearance and language capability, to name just a few. These roadblocks have nothing to do with an individual's ability to perform or to do the job. Organizations do not have written policies that preach discrimination, but sometimes an individual's prejudice can lead to one form of discrimination or another.

Employers rigidly seeking content expertise may exclude candidates with excellent process and transferable skills who might otherwise be superior. An opportunity for a buyer of children's wear may not be open to someone with a background in ladies' or men's wear. As a candidate your responsibility is to iterate and reiterate the transferability of your skills.

In job search mode, it is important to emphasize the relevancy of your qualifications and overcome the barriers from whatever source they may derive. Many of the roadblocks can be dismantled with determination and clarity of purpose. Your task is to build an argument to overcome the barriers and get to the next step. Once you have obtained a job, your next order of business is to keep it.

Hopefully, as you work through the steps outlined in this book, you gain insight into the evolving workplace and how your personality can enhance or limit your success.

We want you to make the most of the opportunity you created for yourself. No job is perfect, but every job is valuable and worth hanging on to for as long as it's rewarding and satisfying. If things start to sour, you have a proven no-nonsense method of success for finding your next job fast. You have a system for building a lifeboat to get you to shore safely.

Good luck, and as we said in the beginning, congratulations!

Index

qualifications, 79
references, 94-96
types of, 81
retainer firms, 108-09
rewards, 38
The Riley Guide, 103, 104, 108
risks, 41
roadblocks, 75-77, 160-61
routine, 42-43

S
salary, 150
schedules, 42-43
screening interviews, 129
search firms
    contingency firms, 109
    employment agencies, 109-10
    retainer firms, 108-09
self-confidence, 76-77
self-doubt, 23-24
self-employment, 74
self-image, 16
selling yourself, 99
    clothing, 144-45
    see also marketing yourself
severance packages, 154
six-step process, 10-11
skills, 22-23, 55
    academic, 61
    design/writing, 59
    finance/accounting, 61
    health professions, 61
    human resources, 61
    information systems, 59-60
    management/administration, 59
    marketing/sales/customer service, 59

    operations, 60
    people professions, 61
    research/engineering, 60
    skilled trades, 61
    support professions, 60-61
    transferability of, 161
    upgrading, 75-76
skills inventory, 59-61
SMACK, 70-71
SMART, 66-68
spouses, 32-34
standards, 39
start, fresh, 40-41
storytelling, 142-43
strategies
    finding employment, 68-69
    negotiating, 157-58
stress, 15, 36-37
stress test interviews, 133-34
structured interviews, 130-31
support, 41
support programs, 44
systematic approach, 66-71

T
target markets, 100
telephone interviews, 128
telephoning, 112-13
thank-you letters, 139-40
Transitions: Making Sense of Life's Changes, 18

U
unemployment insurance, 44
unstructured interviews, 132
US job banks, 103-04